"It is incredibly painful to walk through life believing that you haven't just made a mistake but you are one. I have known the deep struggle of my own shame story, and Mariela is the friend you need to guide you from a place of hiding in fear to the place of standing and declaring the truth of who God says you are. Through her story of surrender in *She Speaks Fire*, Mariela will encourage you to step forward into all God has prepared for you and remind you that what you've been through is not who you are."

—ASHLEY MORGAN JACKSON, BESTSELLING AUTHOR, SPEAKER, AND WRITER FOR PROVERBS 31 MINISTRIES

"Mariela's words are truly a work of art, and this book is a canvas I'll proudly display in my home because of the impact it made on my heart. This is one of those books you'll tell your friends, 'You *have* to read this!' The poetic relatability and profound truth of the Gospel drips from her pen, and I exhaled, wept, smiled and laughed throughout these pages. She has given me a freedom from shame and a boldness in my testimony I didn't even know was missing! As a friend, I know that Mariela not only has a heart of gold but will keep it real with you when needed. What a gift she is, and what a gift this work of art is. WOW!"

—AINSLEY BRITAIN, AUTHOR OF *DON'T DATE A BOOBOO DUDE*

"Mariela is not only an overcomer but she is gifted and anointed to help others overcome every obstacle they face in Christ. Mariela will help reclaim your identity and kick shame in the face in *She Speaks Fire*. She's transparent with her struggles and empathetic in her approach to help you overcome yours. *She Speaks Fire* is full of biblical revelation that'll set your soul on fire. This is one of those books every Christian needs to read and have an extra copy to give to a friend in need."

—BRITTNI DE LA MORA, AUTHOR, SPEAKER, AND COFOUNDER OF LOVE ALWAYS MINISTRIES

"It is incredibly painful to walk through life believing that you haven't just made a mistake but you are one. I have known the deep struggle of my own shame story, and Mariela is the friend you need to guide you from a place of hiding in fear to the place of standing and declaring the truth of who God says you are. Through her story of surrender in *She Speaks Fire*, Mariela will encourage you to step forward into all God has prepared for you and remind you that what you've been through is not who you are."

—ASHLEY MORGAN JACKSON, BESTSELLING AUTHOR, SPEAKER, AND WRITER FOR PROVERBS 31 MINISTRIES

"Mariela's words are truly a work of art, and this book is a canvas I'll proudly display in my home because of the impact it made on my heart. This is one of those books you'll tell your friends, 'You *have* to read this!' The poetic relatability and profound truth of the Gospel drips from her pen, and I exhaled, wept, smiled and laughed throughout these pages. She has given me a freedom from shame and a boldness in my testimony I didn't even know was missing! As a friend, I know that Mariela not only has a heart of gold but will keep it real with you when needed. What a gift she is, and what a gift this work of art is. WOW!"

—AINSLEY BRITAIN, AUTHOR OF *DON'T DATE A BOOBOO DUDE*

"Mariela is not only an overcomer but she is gifted and anointed to help others overcome every obstacle they face in Christ. Mariela will help reclaim your identity and kick shame in the face in *She Speaks Fire*. She's transparent with her struggles and empathetic in her approach to help you overcome yours. *She Speaks Fire* is full of biblical revelation that'll set your soul on fire. This is one of those books every Christian needs to read and have an extra copy to give to a friend in need."

—BRITTNI DE LA MORA, AUTHOR, SPEAKER, AND COFOUNDER OF LOVE ALWAYS MINISTRIES

Praise for *She Speaks Fire*

"*She Speaks Fire* is more than just a book—it's an awakening. Like a friend, Mariela powerfully guides readers from the oppressive weight of shame to the liberating warmth of God's embrace. In a world where shame silently grips the hearts of many, this book emerges as an essential beacon of hope, shedding light on the enduring truth of God's love. With profound biblical teaching and a riveting personal testimony, Mariela's words have the power to fan the embers of your faith, drawing you irresistibly closer to the Father's heart."

—BRITTANY MAHER, FOUNDER AND PRESIDENT OF HER TRUE WORTH AND BESTSELLING AUTHOR

"In a time where people are desperate for authentic voices to lead them towards eternal hope, Mariela invites us to a garden filled with the redemption, grace, and truth of Jesus and His Word. Whether you've followed her words on social media or you're meeting her for the very first time, you will find yourself leaning into her story and comforted by how it weaves into your own—you aren't alone. This book is an invitation to healing and freedom to throw off shame, guilt, and condemnation and walk towards a Father who makes an Eden out of our wilderness."

—NATALIE RUNION, BESTSELLING AUTHOR AND FOUNDER OF RAISED TO STAY

"If there was a scheme of the enemy that could take us all out, it would be shame. The enemy of our souls knows our hiding stunts our healing. So I am beyond hopeful for the freedom Mariela has given us access to in this book. These words are holy weapons that will equip us to go to battle and win. Lean in, gals."

—TONI COLLIER, SPEAKER, PODCAST HOST, AND AUTHOR OF *BRAVE ENOUGH TO BE BROKEN*

Contents

The Seed of Shame

When Shame First Spoke My Name

Did you know that one word from God can make dead things come back to life?

I had a pulse at twenty-eight, but I was dead inside. An autopsy would have declared that I had been killed by shame and its best friend and accomplice, guilt, who supplied additional details of all my sordid past mistakes.

I should have died, but I didn't.

Fast-forward to today and you'll find a woman who is very much alive. In fact, I'm not only alive with breath in my lungs, but I've also got a story in my heart to tell. I consider myself somewhat of a shame expert, not because of my formal education or because I've done extensive research, but because I'm a survivor of shame, a weapon that is claiming the lives and callings of so many people.

I never thought I would author a book, especially this

book. I don't have the ordinary cookie-cutter Christian experience, and that's been the root of much of my shame to this day. Shame has lingered with me all my life, much like the smell of a good ol' fish fry that lingers in your living room for days after a family gathering. It's in the air all around you, but you don't know how to get rid of it. Shame stinks like that until we get good and tired of its rancid smell. Whether you're carrying shame knowingly or unknowingly, it still reeks from your spirit, your language, and your life. There ain't enough Febreze in the world to cover the stench of shame, so we learn to live with it until we can't tell the difference between a good whiff of freedom and the foul odor of humiliation.

I spent nearly three decades living but not feeling alive. When I was twenty-eight I sat in front of a pile of drugs in a room thick with the stench of guilt. I remember thinking, *If I get high one more time, I'm going to die before my thirtieth birthday.* I was depressed, tired, and hopeless. I could feel my heart pounding inside my chest as though it were trying to escape my body the way I was trying to escape my own pain.

I didn't want to feel anymore.

I didn't want to think anymore.

I just wanted to rest.

How did I get to this point?

Nobody just wakes up one day and decides to take a stroll down the road of addiction. Nor does one walk out of one's home and decide to adopt toxic behaviors to cope with pain and failures. But there I was, trapped in a cycle I did not know how to escape. I had no idea why I felt or thought the way I did, but I knew I was not in a good place. To understand how I got to a place where I didn't even recognize myself, I had to go back to the day shame started talking to me. Shame had been talking a good game for decades, and the more it talked, the more silent I became because I had no idea how to respond. How could I know? I was only ten when I first succumbed to shame, and back then, I knew absolutely nothing about it or the lessons it teaches. But I was about to learn.

The Party That Never Happened

It was 1997, and I was entering that impressionable tween age where I was losing my baby fat but still hanging on to chubby cheeks that only my family considered cute. The boys my age found me anything *but* cute, and the girls were too busy judging me to consider *any part* of me cute. The innocence of my childhood met the harsh reality of life, and I realized loud and clear that the world didn't love me or want me the way my family did. I wasn't ready or prepared for my rose-colored glasses to be ripped off my face by jealousy, insecurities, and immaturity. I was about to turn double digits and get a double dose of how quickly young dreams can crumble.

A day (I blocked out which one) in February 1997 will forever be one of the worst days of my life. I am the youngest of nine girls, and the last three of us were born only eleven months apart from each other.

This means two of us are the same age for a few weeks until the older one has a birthday. (For those of you doing the math, yup, my mama was pregnant for three years straight.) Being so close in age and birth means many things, but the most notable is that our birthdays land within the same two months of the year. In our case those months are January and February, and I never looked forward to them. As much as I hated those shared birthday months, I also knew I wasn't being shortchanged because my family was never short on love.

My daddy, who was my primary caregiver after my parents' divorce, modeled to me that I could do anything I put my mind to, and I had no reason to doubt him. My mom, with whom I got to spend summer vacation and other school breaks, smothered me with love when I was with her. My sisters babied me and always knew my needs before I ever did, which meant my needs were met the moment they arose, without a single word from me.

I was loved by my family.

I was provided for by my dad.

I was affirmed by my mom.

I was seen by my sisters.

My world was safe, and I knew my place in it.

How could anything possibly go wrong?

That year, instead of the normal dinner outing followed by our favorite ice cream malt—a tradition in our household—my two sisters and I decided that we should have a party together, which would be the first birthday party I had ever had. I remember eagerly writing each friend's name on my festive little invitations. I wrote the words "You're invited" so big it seemed as though each letter was screaming at the one into whose hands it landed.

I could hardly sleep the night before I handed them out, envisioning what my first birthday party would be like. I imagined balloons, cake, and friends and family laughing. I giggled at the idea of everyone looking at me and singing "Happy Birthday" while secretly hoping someone would smash my face into the cake as I'd seen at a few other parties. I was so excited! I went to school with invitations in hand and started giving them to all my friends. Since I was in the fourth grade, that meant I pretty much handed one out to anyone I'd ever had a conversation with because I didn't want to leave anybody out. Everyone was invited!

Two weeks passed, and the day for our party finally arrived. I put on my favorite outfit for my big day—my cream-colored top with a picture of Simba and Nala (from *The Lion King*) that flared out with a ruffle at the bottom and made me feel girly. My stylish tan biker shorts, decorated with little lions, gave me the margin to freely run and play without the hindrance of wearing a dress. I felt cute. I felt confident. I was ready for my big day.

We arrived at the Family Fun Center and were greeted by the loud noise and flashing lights of the arcade games and everyone enjoying them. I saw the Ferris wheel, bumper cars, and mini golf course in the distance and could hardly wait to rip and run around that place with all my friends. My family was escorted to the party room, where three long tables sat waiting to be occupied by our guests. My sisters and I each had our own table, adorned with balloons and our own cake sitting in the center, ready for when it was time to blow out the candles.

The party started at noon, and my sisters' friends were more punctual than mine, some arriving early. I watched as their guests trickled in and their tables started filling up with gifts. I watched as they jumped up and down and greeted each new arrival with a hug and promise of the fun that would soon follow. I watched as my sisters handed each guest their own cup of tokens so they could play in the arcade.

Twelve o'clock came and went.

One o'clock came and went.

Two o'clock came and went.

And not one of my friends showed up.

Not one.

There I sat, alone at my table, surrounded by cups of unclaimed tokens for friends who never came.

Had I done something wrong?

Feelings of guilt and shame consumed me, but I didn't know exactly why. Surely this had to be my fault; it was something I had done. *I'm bad. I'm ugly. Everyone hates me. I don't have any real friends. Everyone probably had something better to do than come to my party . . .* The narrative went on and on in my mind.

I felt embarrassed, hurt, and exposed as those around me looked at me with compassion accompanied by unintentional pity and the unspoken uncertainty of what to do next. With my head down I summoned every ounce of strength I had in my ten-year-old body to hold back the tears that wanted to flow just like the accusations of worthlessness did in my mind.

And at that moment, I made a choice.

A choice that seemed more familiar to me than anything else.

It came naturally to me.

I made the decision to cover myself and hide behind a smile that could deflect any accusation that I was anything but happy and okay in that very moment.

I decided that the pain of being seen was more costly than the pain I was currently in, so hidden places became my habitation.

Have you ever wanted to just disappear and not be seen? That was me. If that's you, you're not alone.

I didn't come out of hiding until eighteen years later,

when my broken, still-ten-year-old heart was introduced to Jesus.

Growing up, I didn't have an adequate understanding of the gospel from Genesis to Revelation, nor did I have years of attending and serving in the church. I remember going to church as a child occasionally with my dad and hearing the choir sing about a God I didn't know or understand but feeling my eyes well up anyway. I would watch as people sang from the deepest parts of their souls—at times, with tears running down their faces—and I would look to my daddy to gauge how I should be responding. There he'd be, with his arms crossed, lips pressed together, heels tapping in cadence to the beat. He didn't cry, but I always sensed his eyes told a story of a long history with the God of whom they sang. I felt God in those moments, but I didn't know why. It wasn't until January 14, 2015, that I began to understand the love I saw in my daddy's eyes all those years ago.

You might assume I was at a church service, conference, or revival meeting when Jesus saved me, but I wasn't. I was alone in my room when I heard God begin to speak to me. As I sat there on the floor, hiding in my shame and afraid of the world around me, He called me, and I heard His voice. This Jesus my daddy knew pulled the curtain back to put the spotlight of His love directly on me in the midst of my darkness. He introduced me to His love—and that changed everything! I was supernaturally delivered from addiction to hard drugs, and I haven't touched them since. If I hadn't lived it, I'd probably think my salvation was more hype than reality. It's the classic salvation story that ends happily ever after, right?

Wrong.

Though I approached the Scriptures, church service, and the secret place of prayer with God with zeal and excitement, I still had a war raging inside me. In discovering Christianity I was freed from so many things and dove headfirst into my purpose. Yet one thing still lingered: shame. The shame that met me for the first time at ten was the same shame that bound me up while I was preaching freedom in Christ to anyone who would listen. As you may know, I am the founder and leader of a women's ministry called She Speaks Fire, which aims to equip women to own their God-given voices and stories for His glory. Much of my mission is to help people answer the call of God on their lives and live with purpose because I spent most of my life thinking I didn't have a purpose.

It wasn't until I met Jesus that I found out who I really was and the reason I was alive. My passion to help others discover this same truth is what drove me to start my ministry. But even the truth that Jesus had set me free from drug abuse, restored my life, and given me purpose wasn't enough to keep me from being paralyzed by shame. It actually drove me deeper into shame because I *knew* I should be free, but I wasn't. My head understood what Jesus had done for me, but I couldn't understand why the revelation of His freedom hadn't reached my heart. I lived in a constant state of fear, regret, and frustration because shame kept me silent when my spirit was on fire to speak.

Countless women, both in person and online, have told me that something has held them back from stepping 100 percent into their God-given call. Not knowing where to start, not knowing what to do, afraid of being rejected, and the list goes on. Something is keeping us from being truly free, and I am convinced that for many of us it's the seed of shame. On my quest to discover why so many in the body of Christ, including me, were not living as free as Jesus came to make us, I ran face-first into my own shame, which continued to try to keep me hidden and isolated from God, myself, and others. The raw truth is, as long as we're on this side of heaven, the seed of shame will try to embed itself in our lives, and if it's not challenged, confronted, and uprooted, it grows and grows and grows like an unchecked weed that chokes the life out of every living thing in a garden.

Just because I wrote a book about shame doesn't mean I'm exempt from it. I've just learned a few lessons along the way that have helped me recognize and remove its seed when it shows up. I have the courage and conviction to speak about it because of the journey the Lord has taken me on in healing my own shame.

Too often we underestimate shame because we don't really understand its meaning. According to *Merriam-Webster*, shame is "a painful emotion caused by consciousness of

guilt, shortcoming, or impropriety."[1] Notice that its definition begins with the word *painful* before it lists any of its
attributes or causes. That alone
should cause us to pay more
attention to the role shame plays
in our lives. The definition goes
on to say this painful emotion has
a cause—a source that opens the
door and rolls out the red carpet
for it. Sometimes *shame* and *guilt*
are used interchangeably, but their

Too often we underestimate shame because we don't really understand its meaning.

very definitions clearly articulate they are not the same.
Guilt tells us *what we've done*, but shame results from guilt
telling us *who we are*.

Shame is not only a conscious mental response, triggering
us to see ourselves in a negative light, but also an involuntary
human emotion we all experience. Regardless of how much
or how little it affects you, shame is a universal disease that
has infected all of humanity. Tied to the knowledge that
we've messed up for the first time or the thousandth time,
our emotions give shame even more legitimacy because we
feel a deep sense of embarrassment and humiliation. Our
minds and our emotions begin to fully convince us that
shame is our identity based on what we *know* we did and
what we *know* we feel.

Desperate for answers in my own battle with shame,
I was led to a book where I believe I found the answers to

many of the questions that plagued me and may be plaguing you too. My biggest question was: *Where did my shame come from, and how can I battle it?*

As I sensed God calling me to go back to the beginning of Scripture to study Adam and Eve's story to better understand my own story, I realized there was a time when shame wasn't a problem and hiding wasn't a thing. This blew my mind in a whole new way, and I began to search for answers on how the serpent was able to deceive mankind out of the perfect garden and get us to engage in an unending game of hide-and-seek with God and others. God showed me what life looked like before shame came onto the scene as He took my eyes off the familiar story of the two trees in the garden and showed me something else I'd never seen before. It is this revelation that serves as the biblical foundation of this book, which you and I will explore and what I refer to as Garden Lessons.

In Genesis 3:1–7 we see how Adam and Eve were drawn away from the perfect love of God and how the enemy manipulated them to compromise in areas where they were once confident. First, the serpent questioned Eve about what God had said and accused Him of lying (vv. 1–4). Then doubt crept into their identity and the trust they had in God (v. 5). Confusion further tainted purpose when Adam and Eve started coveting something that was not theirs (v. 6). Next, just as they do with us, lies and deception influenced what Eve saw with her physical eyes (v. 6). And just like Eve's did, our perspectives can shift when we look at God's boundaries as a punishment instead of protection (v. 6). Adam and Eve, once free from shame, became slaves, driven to sew together fig leaves to cover up their shame (v. 7).

Maybe you are like me and have read the creation account but never saw the lessons God was trying to teach to protect, cover, and lead us from shame to freedom. In my desperation to be free, God used the garden in Genesis as a classroom to teach me eight Garden Lessons from the perfect world He created, which was free from shame. These were lessons on

identity,
purpose,
community,
approval,
boundaries,
senses,
lies, and
nakedness.

These areas represent the enemy's favorite stomping grounds when it comes to shame, and each lesson moves us toward freedom. Looking to Scripture as our guide, we see the first experience with shame just two chapters after God created Adam, Eve, and the garden of Eden (Genesis 3:7). Now, if you've never heard of Adam and Eve, or you haven't heard their names since Sunday school as a kid, you may have missed some grown-up truths that came from two people who are very much like you and me.

So what changed in the beginning chapters of Genesis? What broke down our perfect relationship with God and moved humanity from naked and unashamed to covering ourselves in fig leaves? How did shame lead our first parents, Adam and Eve, away from the utopia of the garden into hiding, and how is shame still controlling us today?

These Garden Lessons reveal that God's intention for us in the garden was always good—but good intentions don't always equal good outcomes when our free will is involved! The full expression of God's love and mercy had to come with the freedom for us to choose; otherwise, we'd always question His identity, His sovereignty, and His integrity.

God chose to create us as sons and daughters who would be bound to His will in love, not as slaves who are bound to His will by force. Love without freedom of choice isn't love at all; it's bondage. God invited Adam and Eve into a perfect, loving relationship and gave them the power to choose—even if that meant they may not make the right choice.

In this book I'm going to walk you through eight Garden Lessons found in the book of Genesis so you can learn how to identify shame in your life, its origins, the atmosphere that fosters and hinders its existence and growth, how it attacks your relationship with God and others, and how it's out to destroy your contentment and purpose. In dissecting the

Genesis account, I have extracted lessons from our first parents and the atmosphere in which shame did not exist. The places where shame attacked Adam and Eve so many years ago are the very same areas where shame attacks us now. As we examine this with intentionality and vulnerability, my sincere hope is that you sense God pointing out how shame has operated in your life up until this moment and hear His voice showing you how to overcome it *His* way so you can truly live a life of freedom.

I've written this book to help you begin the journey of uncovering your own shame. If you've never experienced the true freedom that comes from God and God alone, you may not even realize how debilitating shame can be. Or maybe you have experienced the freedom God offers, but what you knew then is not what you know now, and you're still battling shame. Maybe your story is a little like Adam's or a little like Eve's and shame has you a little more than deceived. As we journey together, I hope you will learn not only to battle your own shame but that your faith will be reignited throughout the pages of this book and you will finish the last page filled with a passion to reclaim your purpose.

I'm convinced the louder I get about how shame operates, the quieter shame becomes. You probably have your own relationship with shame, and I hope you get loud and honest about how it has played you, lied to you, manipulated you, and all the while, you didn't even know it. Until now.

When we get real, real change can happen. When we look in the mirror and do not turn away, we see more than we deny. When we stop pretending to be something we're not, we can become and embrace who we really are. I love that for me, and I love that for you.

When we get real, real change can happen.

First, let's tackle shame head-on. What is it? Where did it come from? And how does it show up in our lives? Let's go back and see how it all began.

Garden Prayer

Father, as I embark on this journey of exposing shame, I come to You in prayer, seeking Your guidance and comfort. I thank You that You are on this journey with me every step of the way, and I stand on Your promise that You will never leave me or forsake me.

I pray that through the pages in this book, I may find the courage to confront my shame and seek healing. Help me let go of anything that may be holding me back and find the strength to move forward with Your love and grace.

Please open my eyes to see myself as You see me, as Your beloved child, who is worthy of being fully seen and fully known. In Jesus' name I pray, amen.

Identity

Identity and the Counterfeit Life

I'll never forget the night I humiliated myself and vowed never to write or speak again.

A close friend with whom I had shared my first poem asked me to share a spoken word at a young adult gathering at church. Halfway through my poem, I completely blanked and forgot all the words. I was so focused on everybody's faces and reactions that I was gripped by fear and stood there like a deer in headlights. I scrambled to find my footing and remember what I was trying to say. Tripping toward the finish line and grappling for breath and composure, I finally got through the piece. Despite the applause surrounding me when I finished, the shame that gripped me as I walked back to my seat is something I still recall vividly. I was overtly aware of everyone staring at me and convinced they were thinking how much of a loser I was, so I kept my head down in humiliation for the rest of the service. I desperately wanted to hide under a rock and never come out again. My identity was tied to being a good spoken word artist, and I had failed at that in front of everyone. I felt completely worthless. However, through that horrible experience, God taught me that if my identity is built on anything outside of Him, I will find myself outside of my security and my purpose and inside the cage of shame.

As someone who has struggled with shame since I was a young girl, I know how it makes us want to run and hide and move in secret. It disguises itself so cunningly that we don't even know when it's in operation. Before God came into my life, shame had the full run of my thoughts, emotions, and decision-making, but I didn't know it. I thought I was in the driver's seat, but when I look back now with wisdom, maturity, and revelation, I can see how I consulted shame as a best friend or therapist before I ever made a move or shed a tear. It was shame that drove me to destructive patterns to escape my reality, and it was shame that had me looking to external things to cover up my constant feelings of guilt. I tried and tried to fill the gap shame left behind, but nothing ever could, and nothing ever would. I was always left empty, lost, hurting, and confused.

Every day, shame would remind me of mistakes I had made, battles I had lost with other people, and ground I couldn't regain within myself. Over and over, shame played on like a familiar song that came to lead me in a dance of pretending, hiding, and people-pleasing so that my flaws were only a passing blur to those who cared to look. I never stopped dancing, hoping no one would see my mistakes and all the guilt I wore. For almost thirty years, with partners like fear, mistrust, and anxiety, I moved and swayed too quickly for others to see the real me. All the while, shame crooned so softly in my ear that only I could hear its lyrics.

You are unloved.

You are unwanted.

You are a failure.

You are a burden.

And then the beat would drop and shame's famous one-liner would echo in my heart: *Nobody would ever miss you if you were gone.*

I had no idea who I was without shame, and I had no idea how to contend with the words of shame that tempted me with death. Can you relate? Maybe shame is telling you the same things, and you don't know how to respond. Although I vowed to remain silent in my shame and humiliation, God gave me new words in His living Word to combat the lies shame whispered in my spirit. I fell in love with His Word, and in it, I found a weapon against shame and its attack on my identity.

Today when my identity is attacked—and it's attacked

often—I stand on God's Word that says that even before I was in my mother's womb, He knew me, and He created me (Psalm 139:13). I look up instead of down and focus on the truth that I am fearfully and wonderfully made in His likeness (v. 14). I hold fast to the truth that I am loved (Romans 8:38–39), I am chosen (1 Peter 2:9), and I am purposed for good works (Ephesians 2:10).

And that's what I want to encourage you to do, because sooner or later, we're all going to have to take a walk back into the garden to find out who we are.

As I learned the first lesson the garden revealed about identity, I realized that the same lies the serpent was telling then, he is still telling now. The game he played on mankind that led God's creation into shame is the same game he still tries to play now to *keep* us in our shame. The serpent didn't just use his cunning deception to *do* something against God's perfect plan; he convinced God's beloved creation to *know* something against God's perfect plan. That's a big difference in strategy. I imagine satan banked on the fact that if he attacked their consciousness, Adam and Eve couldn't unknow what they now knew. I wonder, however, if he considered how Adam and Eve would respond to their nakedness and how generations after them would still respond the same way: "At that moment their eyes were opened, and they suddenly felt shame at their nakedness. So they sewed fig leaves together to cover themselves" (Genesis 3:7 NLT).

They dressed themselves with fig leaves because they

knew God was going to come looking for them in the cool of the day. Even in their sin and shame, they knew what they had done couldn't change God's desire to spend the last moments of the day with them in relationship and in fellowship. There was no question for them that He would want to talk with them, know about their day, and just be near them. So they used fig leaves to cover themselves and quickly realized those skimpy leaves didn't have the ability to cover them sufficiently or take away their shame.

The moment Adam and Eve covered their nakedness, they took on a new identity. And not a God-given one but one *they* gave themselves. They were no longer free in their true identity as image bearers of God; they were now naked and ashamed. Their newfound awareness caused them to hide themselves from each other and from the God who created them without shame. While we may not have fig leaves handy today, we still reach for our own figurative leaves.

We use these counterfeit identities to hide our shame, and they are different for each person. Some of us cover ourselves in anger and hide behind defensiveness. Others procrastinate or live out a career, marriage, or vocation that someone else chose for them. Our fig leaves may be the addictions and habits that hide the real pain we are carrying. What's even scarier and more disheartening to admit is that these twenty-first-century fig leaves are too often praised, rewarded, and coveted in our world.

For example, some people's fig leaves manifest in the

form of intellect. They are so smart and can explain even the most complex of subjects or experiences with such ease and poetic utterance that even those who despise wisdom want to learn. They are praised for it. They excel in their field, and people covet their intelligence and influence—but what others probably don't know is that the person they admire could be battling feelings of worthlessness and incompetence. They have simply created a false self based on what they can achieve or articulate to deal with the feelings of inadequacy that they really experience.

Another modern-day fig leaf that we don't talk about enough is one too many church folk wear while they worship and preach. Our churches are filled with too many believers who have lost themselves to service and religious activities but are hiding the truth that they don't have an authentic relationship with God that doesn't revolve around *doing*. However, religious people can't escape the intolerable effects of shame by relying on serving, praying, fasting, or meditating any more than the rich, the educated, or the successful can find their identity solely in what they've acquired. I am convinced that shame is at the root of why we've seen a rise in great, anointed leaders falling from positions of influence in the church at large. It's so easy to hide behind public gifts and anointing and ignore the private battles within. Religious practices that stem from trying to be "holy" while covering up faults and foibles aren't ever going to be big enough to cover up shame because fig leaves were never part of God's original design for us.

Before I come for all our fig leaves, I want to connect the dots on why we choose these even though history and experience have shown us they don't work. Like any other feeling, shame is an emotion that is first processed and felt in the heart; then we respond based on our consciousness of that emotion. For example, let's say you feel sad. The feeling of sadness is first felt in your heart and then elicits a physical response in the form of frowning, crying, or having a meltdown as you become conscious of what you're feeling.

This same process is how shame crept into Adam's and Eve's hearts, resulting in the physical response of sewing fig leaves together to hide their consciousness of sin. This is the same process satan tries to use with us today. But because God didn't intend for us to carry shame, our physical bodies don't have the innate capacity to accept shame. So we reach for fig leaves to hide what we're feeling. Little white lies may cause a small amount of shame, so we grab for a handful of fig leaves, while "big" shameful situations, like exposed public sins of disgrace, make us reach for all the leaves on the fig tree! Think of it like this: you'll need a couple of fig leaves for stealing a cookie from the cookie jar, but you'll need a truckload of fig leaves for sleeping with the married baker.

The more we reach for fig leaves, the more they end up becoming part of our identity. We don't just need them to hide our sin; we need them to maintain the lie that we're not hurting, lost, or afraid. We don't just hide behind them; we graft our hearts to them so that we're never vulnerable without them. We have chosen them repeatedly until we've forgotten how to choose anything else—like the truth. The fig leaves we reached for in our adolescent years won't last through our adult years, nor will the ones we chose in our coldest, darkest seasons withstand the heat of our warmest, brightest seasons. Eventually, we'll need to sew new fig leaves, and the cycle of hiding will continue.

Drugs, sex, ministry, busyness, and charisma have been some of my favorite fig leaves to grab in my own cycle of shame and hiding. Can you relate? When was the last time you looked for a fig leaf when you wanted to hide or disappear out of guilt and humiliation? How many fig leaves do you have from last season that aren't fitting in this season? Have you sewn a fig leaf over your own mouth to silence yourself, your thoughts, your dreams, or your opinions out of fear of being rejected? What fig tree do you have growing in the garden of your heart just in case someone gets too close to the you you're trying to hide? Friend, we may all have different answers to these questions, but shame is the root, and covering and hiding are the fruits.

The Weight That's Hard to Lose

I started starving myself when I was sixteen after miserably failing the Weight Watchers program that I'd begged my dad to let me join right after my thirteenth birthday. Food had been a source of solace and comfort ever since I first felt the sting of shame on my tenth birthday, and I just couldn't seem to find enough fig leaves to hide all the weight I was carrying. I was barely five foot three and more than two hundred pounds, but the weight of humiliation and embarrassment I was carrying on the inside added even more. Others saw a two-hundred-pound thirteen-year-old, but I saw myself as weighing well over three hundred pounds. If you can remember even a moment of junior high, you know those numbers can earn you a big fat F in the categories of coolness and acceptance.

In school I knew a grandiose and likable personality could cover my scale numbers, so my charm and charisma became my go-to fig leaves to keep from being rejected. However, this only hurt me and added more shame to my emotional scale. See, my fig leaves of charm meant I never had a problem making friends or being liked. I won Best Personality in middle school and Best All-Around in high school and was the high school homecoming queen. I was very popular, but I didn't see myself as others did. Still, although I felt horrible inside, my fig leaves covered me well—except with the boys. I didn't get attention from boys in high school like the skinnier girls did, so when a guy asked me to be his secret girlfriend because I wasn't hot and he didn't want his friends to make fun of him, I didn't argue. More shame, more pounds on the scale.

So there I was, at a Weight Watchers center in humiliation

and shame, lined up behind women two and three times my age. It was clear to me that age wasn't connected to our universal struggle to love ourselves. I felt just as lost in this older crowd as I did in a crowd of my peers. I hated who I was in both settings. To make matters worse, no one was talking to me about the internal extra weight I was carrying or giving me strategies to lose it. I was barely a teenager, but I was morbidly overweight emotionally and physically.

Each week we lined up, one behind the other like cattle, clutching the little white books we were given that recorded our weight. I hated that book. I hated what it represented, the secrets it held, and the scorecard it carried. My hands would sweat as I held on to that book because, to me, it had the power to determine my worth based on the number that popped up on the scale.

Am I skinnier than I was last week?

Did I count my food points correctly?

Will the scale go up because of those Flamin' Hot Cheetos I ate?

I am going to be so embarrassed if I gained weight.

Those were just some of the thoughts that ran through my head as I took one step closer to the scale I believed held the authority to determine if I was worth loving.

Looking back, it's crazy to think an inanimate, silent square on the ground could hold so much power over me. But in my world, it carried more influence than my best friend, held more secrets than my diary, and triggered more emotion than the trauma caused by my tenth birthday party. Ever since that horrific day, I had seen myself and my world differently. I had lost an innocent confidence that made me feel secure in any situation and now found myself hiding in a garden of food. That stupid scale opened my eyes and showed me I was naked every week by putting a number in front of my face that I couldn't hide from.

And so the destructive pattern of dieting, agonizing about food, and binge eating in private eventually landed me face up on an operating table covered by a sheet of fig leaves.

When I failed at all the attempts to lose the internal and external weight, surgery became my next cover-up. By my early twenties, I had spent over a decade of my life attempting to fix myself because my identity was rooted in the "when Is" and "will bes."

When I lose weight, I *will be* lovable.
When I fit in those jeans, I *will be* beautiful.
When I think I look good, I *will be* wanted.

Not realizing that in God's eyes I was already valuable, I rooted my identity in the standards of our culture and what I thought I needed to be, which kept me chasing something outside myself to find myself. My identity had been replaced by "Ms. Do Something to Become Something."

Isn't it the same for many of us?

You may never have struggled with your body image

(lucky you!), but I know without a doubt you have been tempted to place your identity in external things.

We have all done so and are continually tempted to do so.

My friend, what are your "when Is" and "will bes"? They may sound something like this:

When I get my degree, I *will be* considered intelligent.
When I am spiritually disciplined, I *will be* loved
    by God.
When I please _____ [fill in name], I *will be* accepted.
When I grow my social media, I *will be* validated in
    my purpose.
When I get connected to the right people, I *will have*
    favor.

The "when Is" and "will bes" lead us right into the cycle of shame because we are placing our identities in something outside of the One who gave us identity in the first place. By default, we have all been born into a system that begs us to take action to justify our position in this world. We have been sold the lie from the beginning of time that if we "do" something, then we will "be" something.

And guess what? It started in the garden: "For God knows that when you eat from it your eyes will be opened, and you will be like God, knowing good and evil" (Genesis 3:5).

The serpent's words to Eve attacked Adam's and Eve's identities by suggesting that they were not already like God, when in fact, the very purpose of their existence was to reflect the image and likeness of God (Genesis 1:26).

The enemy knew if he could get Adam and Eve to question their identities, he could get them away from trusting God. Our trust in God is critical to understanding the identity questions that bombard us as we navigate through life. Our internal conversation about identity may encompass a variety of questions about purpose, motivation, and significance, but identity always leads us back to one question. "In the most general terms *identity* refers to one's answer to the question, Who am I?"[2]

Shame was not present in the garden when Adam's and Eve's identities were rooted in God, and the same is true for us today. You aren't defined by what you do or don't do. You weren't created in the image of your own actions. You aren't measured by your last conversation, decision, or deed. Imagine what every day would be like if decisions and actions were life lessons marked by growth instead of by shame. This vantage point would allow us to see ourselves how God sees us rather than how satan sees us.

I think it's only fair to mention and important to acknowledge that sometimes we root our identities not just in who *we* think we need to be but in what others have spoken over us as well.

I grew up in an all-white neighborhood in California and for most of my life was one of maybe three Black students in my grade. Being called a monkey and a jigaboo was a normal occurrence and something I learned to ignore like the chirp of a smoke detector in need of new batteries. The name-calling was annoying, but it didn't stop me from living. I would love to attest that my ability to move on from these painful comments came from a strong sense of self-confidence and worth that wouldn't be unnerved by racist slurs and demeaning jokes. But I would be lying. I endured the brutality of others' words because I didn't believe in myself and my worth enough to say, "Stop." As a young person, I didn't know I had a voice to speak out and tell others that what they were saying wasn't true. I was too scared of rejection, even by people who were hurting me, so I stayed silent.

What have people spoken over you? Did you go back to college because someone called you stupid? Have you spent your life chasing success because someone called you poor? Do you avoid asking for help and pretend to be strong because someone called you weak?

We can't find true purpose until we come to the foot of the cross.

No matter how tirelessly we work to cover up the words we've heard from ourselves or others, we can't find true purpose until we come to the foot of the cross, where we find our real identity. It's there where we trade in our fig leaves for God's covering of redemption, grace, and restoration. It's in that moment, when we understand

14

our true identity as who He created us to be, that all other voices fall silent. It's there where we come face-to-face with His perspective instead of our own.

We all have different stories, and we all have different fig leaves. Some of us use our outgoing personalities, our job titles, our kids, our partners, our social status, materialism, success, and dare I say religious accolades to cover up the truth that *we don't know who we are without those things.* At least that is what it was like and is like for me.

I didn't know who I was without my coverings, so I couldn't figure out which part of my identity was secure and which part I still had to work for. Once shame starts to dance with our identity, satan knows we'll work *for* our identity instead of working *from* it. There is a vast difference between the two. One admits our total dependence on God while the other declares our independence from God.

Think of it this way: If you're an intern in a company without a paycheck, you're going to work as hard as you can to position yourself to be hired with benefits and pay. But if you're the owner of that same company, you're going to work differently because you're not trying to earn what you already have. (Notice I said, "work differently," not "work less.") Satan wants us to believe we're interns in God's kingdom so that we keep striving for a position, paycheck, and benefits. We're not interns. We're co-owners with more benefits than we can ever imagine.

The Tension Between Real and Counterfeit

If you're reading this book, I'm assuming you've sat through a sermon or two about satan and his lies about who you are in Christ. We have all heard messages on identity, and I'm not here to give you another one without also giving you depth and context on how to live out that identity outside the church walls. Sometimes "identity" is seen as a church word and preached about as a religious concept only.

But can I be honest?

I know what it's like to sit in church and hear "You are more than a conqueror in Christ Jesus!" but feel defeated 99 percent of the time. I know what it's like to hear "God has not given us a spirit of fear!" but be paralyzed by fear more days than I can count. I know what it's like to wonder if there is something wrong with me because I know what the preacher is saying is true, but the reality of my life tells a different story. So I try harder, and I do more, and I eventually grow weary from my own efforts, which perpetuates the cycle of shame.

Can you relate, or is it just me?

I think this is a point of tension for a lot of believers, if we are honest enough to admit it. Living in this tension myself for a good portion of my journey in Christ, I kept asking God what I was missing, and He challenged my understanding about my identity.

And I want to challenge yours.

Could it be that your identity has much less to do with you and much more to do with God?

Could it be that it's not a matter of believing more in who you are in Christ but believing more in the God who knows who you are—the God who created you and knows your identity?

Although the two can sound the same, they are very different. One puts us in the place of power and the other puts us in a place of surrender. One puts the focus on us, while the other puts the focus on God.

When we believe that God is good, trustworthy, just, faithful, true, compassionate, kind, and who He says He is, then believing Him results in seeing ourselves more clearly. The more accurately we can see ourselves, the less likely we are to believe the lies the enemy tries to sell us.

Have you ever looked someone in the eye and caught a glimpse of your own reflection? To be able to see yourself in someone else's eyes means you must be close to that person and share a level of intimacy. You're not hiding from him or her. You're openly and freely showing that person all that you are and vice versa.

I mention reflection because when we talk about identity, we are often referred to as the apple of God's eye. We get this from the psalmist as he prayed, "Keep me as the apple of your eye; hide me in the shadow of your wings" (Psalm 17:8). According to the *Holman Illustrated Bible Dictionary*, the phrase "apple of the eyes" is an "English expression that refers to the pupil of the eye and therefore to something very precious."[3]

In saying "keep me," the psalmist was teaching us our position before God as His children. God watches over us so closely and intently that if we were to look into His eyes, we would see ourselves.

Could it be that the only way to properly see ourselves is through the reflection in God's eyes?

In the physical, we are only able to see ourselves through a reflection in a mirror. We can imagine what we look like, we can describe what we see in our minds, but until we see our own reflection, the images in our imaginations are all we have to stand on. We might ask people how we look, and we listen to their responses to confirm or deny what we see in our mind's eye until we get confirmation for ourselves when we look in a mirror.

All those years ago, I saw myself in the numbers on the scale at Weight Watchers. I was determining who I was based on how overweight I was. I was trying to find my value in the reflection I saw on the LED screen at my feet. I didn't know that to understand my identity I needed to look up to God, not down to the ground at a number on a scale.

Could it be that we have been depending on our own ability to know who we are without seeing who we are in the reflection of God's eyes?

Simply hearing who you are in Christ and knowing who

you are in Christ means nothing until you gaze at the Father and see your own reflection as He gazes back at you. It's from that posture that you go from *knowing* who you are to *believing* who He says you are.

In knowing Him we experience a love that we have never known. A love that can cast out every fear and lead even the hardest of hearts to repentance (1 John 4:18). As we gaze upon Him, we see a love that willingly lays down His life so that His children can live (1 John 3:16). A love that promises never to leave us or forsake us (Hebrews 13:5). A love that is just, loyal, faithful, and true. A love that isn't found on a scale, in a title, or in the words of someone else.

And from that place you can confidently say, "I am loved by God." Not because a preacher told you and it became knowledge in your mind, but because you gazed upon God and saw yourself in His eyes.

Simply *knowing* your identity is not enough because knowledge can become a false faith. We must come to the place of intimacy with God, where what He sees is what we see. We must come so close to Him that we can differentiate satan's lies from God's truth. Many of us know all the Christian lingo and can spout off information we've heard from preachers or read in our Bibles, but until that information becomes revelation, it will be useless. Going to a pool won't make us swimmers until we get all the way in the water and learn how to swim. Similarly, we must get in all the way with God and learn how to become submerged in

We may not always keep our focus on Him, but His focus will always be on us.

His revelation of who we are. We can't take someone else's word on how deep the water is or how warm it feels while sitting on the edge; we have to get all the way in. As we're learning to swim, we may not stay afloat the entire time, but God will never let us drown either. We may not always keep our focus on Him, but His focus will always be on us.

Ditching the Leaves

How do we get our focus back if we've lost it somewhere along the way between the garden and today?

In the garden of Eden, when humanity stood naked and unashamed, Adam and Eve were God-focused and not self-focused. It wasn't until their focus was taken off God and put on themselves that they realized they were naked, felt shame, and resorted to covering themselves with fig leaves. God gave us identity from the beginning by declaring in the presence of all creation, "Let us make man in our image, according to our likeness" (Genesis 1:26 csb).

To be created in the image of God means we are to mirror the spiritual nature of the Father, Son, and Holy Spirit. To be created in His likeness means we are to mirror His function here on earth. The identity of humanity has always been to reflect the beauty and the complexity of God. Since the fall, the only way for you and me to reconnect humanity with God's identity is for us to come out of hiding and into Christ. "In Christ" is a phrase commonly used by church people but not always commonly understood. When we say "in Christ," it means our identity is now intertwined and interdependent on Him and all that He is. It's to say that we are no longer in our mess, in our shame, or in hiding. We share in His perfect, blameless, and flawless identity, and we no longer need the fig leaves we once wore.

In Christ our identity has been fully redeemed. We are given the gift of being able to stand naked and unashamed once again before God and each other because our focus has returned to its rightful place—on Him. The shame that comes from being self-focused causes us to put our identities in those things we use to cover our nakedness, but Christ removes our fig leaves and covers us with Himself.

In Christ our identity is no longer in our public successes or failures.

In Christ our identity is no longer in our children or our inability to have them.

In Christ our identity is no longer in our jobs or in unemployment.

In Christ our identity is no longer in our social statuses or our sense of rejection.

In Christ our identity is no longer in our financial abundance or lack.

In Christ our identity is no longer in our spouses or our singleness.

No, no, no!

In Christ, our identity is no longer in anything outside of Him, and it's from that place that we can confidently claim the truth about who we are.

In Him

you are a new creation (2 Corinthians 5:17),

you are chosen by God (Ephesians 1:11),

you are His child (John 1:12),

you are His friend (John 15:15),

you are holy and righteous (Ephesians 4:24),

you are the temple of His Holy Spirit (1 Corinthians 6:19–20),

you are known (Jeremiah 1:5),

you are created in the image of God (Genesis 1:27),

you are forgiven and redeemed (Ephesians 1:7),

you are appointed to bear fruit (John 15:16),

you are blameless (Ephesians 1:4), and

you are free from condemnation (Romans 8:1).

Shall I keep going?

You are sanctified (1 Corinthians 1:2),

you are justified (Roman 5:1),

you are led by the Spirit of God (Romans 8:14),

you are not moved by what you see (2 Corinthians 4:18),

you are daily overcoming the devil (1 John 4:4),

you are the righteousness of God (2 Corinthians 5:21),

you are an overcomer by the blood of the Lamb and
the word of your testimony (Revelation 12:11),

you are blessed with all spiritual blessings (Ephesians
1:3),

you are kept in safety wherever you go (Psalm 91:11),
and

you are establishing God's kingdom here on earth
(Matthew 16:19).

I'll stop here, but know that this is barely scratching the surface.

I invite you to explore the Bible on your own for more scriptures about identity so that you can discover what God is saying to you personally. I've gotten you started, but there is so much more written in His Word for you!

If you remember anything from what I've said about identity, I want you to remember this: the attack on your identity will always be rooted in the temptation to question if God's Word is true and if your identity in Christ is enough to overcome your shame and reclaim your purpose.

How you answer those two ifs will determine whether you are carried away as a prisoner of war on the battlefield of shame or you are victorious over its attempt to take you captive.

If you prefer victory, then get ready to learn how to defeat the enemy and reclaim your purpose, calling, and passion. If you don't believe victory is possible, stay with me. Continue this journey and let's discover together if where you are today is where you'll stay. You may be surprised by the end of this book to see how far you've come.

In God's original plan we were intended to wear His freedom, not fig leaves of shame. If we're going to live out His purpose for our lives, we're going to have to believe we are more than leaf-wearers. Keep reading and let's keep learning together.

Garden Reflection

Take a moment to think, pray, and reflect on the truths you've learned about identity and respond to the following questions. As you begin to be honest with your answers, what is the Holy Spirit saying to you?

- Which parts of your life are authentic and which parts are counterfeit?
- How have experiences, others' opinions, and social or cultural stigmas played a role in creating a counterfeit identity? What would you gain or lose by letting go of this pseudoidentity?
- What fig leaves are you using currently to cover

yourself? Have you sensed the Holy Spirit asking you to shed them? What is a first step you can take to obey His leading?

At the end of each Garden Lesson, you will find a declaration of truth to speak over yourself as you discover the fire in your voice to battle shame, reignite your faith, and claim your purpose. Here's the one for this lesson:

SPEAKING FIRE INTO YOUR IDENTITY

I declare that my identity is firmly rooted in Christ and shame is not my portion [Isaiah 61:7]. I am fully loved, fully accepted, and fully complete in Him, and I choose to believe I am who God says I am. I will trust only in the assurance of His Word for my identity because it is life to those who believe [Romans 8:16–17, 35–39].

Purpose

Passion, Pursuit, and Other Pitfalls

One day, when I was nineteen, I was desperate, hysterical, and terrified. Driving home in my car, I bawled my eyes out, on the verge of a full-blown panic attack, and I needed someone to talk to. I was out of control. I was shook. I couldn't believe what had just happened to me and urgently needed someone to help me process it.

On a warm summer night, I was leaving a fun event without a care or concern in my mind, when out of nowhere three girls attacked me. All three were complete strangers to me, and they sat on the hood of my car, waiting for me like a pack of wolves scouting their prey. There was nowhere for me to go and nowhere for me to run, so I pressed onward, hoping there could potentially be some resolution found in my words. I had never been in a fight before, but my instincts were telling me this was not going to end well. Before I could even open my mouth to form a sentence, all three jumped off the hood of my car and charged at me. One girl was hitting me from the front, another was pulling my hair from the back, and the third decided that kicking was more her style.

Getting jumped by three people was a heck of a way to be initiated into the rough-and-tumble club. At that point in my life, I had been involved with some shady people, and these three musketeers were sent to give me a warning, using pain in one hand and humiliation in the other. As I was getting beat up and doing my best to defend myself, I pleaded with them to stop; instead of stopping, they laughed and used my supplications as fuel to go harder.

Finally, after what seemed like an eternity, the blows ceased, and I was left in the middle of the street with my clothes torn and blood splattered across my face like paint on a canvas. I watched as the excess dripped onto the street as though my blood were the perfect material for creating a masterpiece on concrete. As I struggled to my feet, I realized that the humiliation hurt much more than the physical wounds.

I felt violated and ashamed.

I got in my car and laid my head on my steering wheel and cried. I cried and I cried and I cried. I grabbed my cell phone and called a friend, but she didn't answer, so I tried someone else. Again, no answer. I desperately needed someone to talk to, so I went down my contact list and just started making calls, hoping someone would answer. I must have made close to ten calls before I finally got a response.

It was sobering to realize that my desperation didn't guarantee someone would pick up the phone. No matter how much I prayed, begged, or cried, I couldn't make someone answer my call. They had to be willing to answer, even if they had no idea what was waiting for them on the other end. Thankfully, my sister answered and walked me through how to get help. To this day I have never been more grateful to have someone answer my call.

I've thought back on that night many times since then, and I have learned to hold a different perspective from the one I did all those years ago. I didn't know it back then, but that night put a spark in my bones for all women who have felt betrayed, in shock, and disoriented with no one to call. That spark was the flicker that would become a full-blown flame of purpose to help women get up from all the humiliating and shaming situations that have left them battered so that they can reignite their faith and reclaim their purpose. My ministry, She Speaks Fire, was conceived in my heart that night. I just didn't know it yet.

Of course, if I had known my purpose and calling were linked to one of my most horrific memories, I wouldn't have wasted so many years striving, working, and searching for it.

In my conversations with hundreds of people through my She Speaks Fire community, I have discovered that Christian culture has complicated the simplicity and authenticity of what it truly means to be called by God. We have put a great emphasis on the idea of being "called" and finding our "purpose," and a false narrative has been established because of it—the narrative being that we must find or discover our calling for ourselves. So many have shared with me that the pressure of trying to figure out their calling and purpose led them into a cycle of shame, anxiety, and depression that became a pitfall of purpose. They felt lost and spent more days than they could count trying to answer the questions, "What is God calling me to do? What is my purpose? What am I supposed to be doing with my life? Did I miss it?"

It wasn't that purpose in and of itself was a pitfall, but the striving, performing, and manufacturing that they thought could give them meaning became their stumbling block. Like me, they had become so obsessed with finding their "calling" that their attention had moved away from the One who'd called them in the first place.

For too many years after I got saved and began to serve in ministry, I struggled with my own pitfall of purpose by thinking I had to do everything and try anything so that I could achieve a sense of fulfillment and purpose. I never once considered looking inward at the work God had been doing in my life since the day I was born. I only looked outside of me, hoping to strive hard enough and perform well enough.

But I missed the mark and lived with the constant doubt that God would have any use for me. What's worse is that I thought this was the way life was *supposed* to be lived. I didn't know there was a time when striving and performance-based living weren't a thing until I read Genesis.

When I read the first two chapters in Genesis—before the serpent showed up in the garden—I can see there was not a doubt or question in Adam or Eve about their purpose and calling. It was the serpent's contrary voice that gave them cause to doubt and question. Scripture teaches us that it was satan, not God, who introduced the idea that who we are and what we have been given is not enough. When I read Genesis 3:4–5 in the story of the fall, I see three truths about the enemy:

1. God is not the originator of discontentment in our contentment; the enemy is.
2. Past or present circumstances are not to blame for confusion in our calling; the enemy is.
3. Experiences are not the source of doubt in God; the enemy is.

Why does that matter? If you and I can see that our purpose and calling don't come with anxiety, confusion, or discontentment, then we can start to subtract what the enemy tries to add.

In the garden the serpent tried to add purpose to Eve. What do I mean by that? When he offered her fruit from the forbidden tree, he was tempting her with a desire outside of God's will for her (Genesis 3:5). The sad thing is that he was tempting her with a desire for knowledge that superseded her intimate connection with God. In other words Eve traded personal relationship with God—the originator of all knowledge and wisdom—to gain knowledge for herself. She walked with God, who withholds no good thing from those He loves and had already provided everything she needed to fulfill her purpose. But because she looked externally instead of internally for purpose, she couldn't see the good God had already given her.

Everything Eve needed was already in her to live out her calling and purpose, and if you are in Christ, the same is true for you.

What's even more incredible about all this is that Adam and Eve's sin couldn't change the purpose and calling that God had given them any more than sin can change your purpose and calling today. Before the fall in Genesis, God gave Adam and Eve clear purpose and calling: "God said to them, 'Be fruitful and multiply; fill the earth and subdue it; have dominion over the fish of the sea, over the birds of the air, and over every living thing that moves on the earth'" (Genesis 1:28 NKJV).

Before Adam and Eve sinned, God told them to fill the earth and have dominion over every part of it. After they sinned, God still wanted them to fill the earth and have dominion over every part of it. He didn't change the plan.

When He found them naked and ashamed, He still talked to Eve about bringing forth children, and He still tasked Adam with ruling over the ground (Genesis 3:16–19). God didn't start talking to them about hustling to get back on track or striving to be perfect again. None of that was in His original plan, and it wasn't in His redemption plan either. He did not change their identity as a response to their sin, and He made sure to say that to Adam and Eve in front of the enemy.

When Adam and Eve hid from God because they realized their shame and heard His footsteps, the serpent wasn't too far away. At one point God turned from His conversation with His son and daughter to address him:

> And He said, "Who told you that you were naked? Have you eaten from the tree of which I commanded you that you should not eat?" Then the man said, "The woman whom You gave to be with me, she gave me of the tree, and I ate." And the LORD God said to the woman, "What is this you have done?" The woman said, "The serpent deceived me, and I ate." So the LORD God said to the serpent: "Because you have done this, you are cursed more than all cattle, and more than every beast of the field; on your belly you shall go, and you shall eat dust all the days of your life." (Genesis 3:11–14 NKJV)

I imagine that crafty serpent kept a cool distance but stayed close enough to hear what punishment Adam and

Eve's sin would bring. He was probably betting that God would rescind Adam and Eve's purpose and exchange it for penalty. That fool was waiting to hear their punishment, waiting to see their purpose stripped from them, and waiting for God's children to lose. But God didn't let that happen. He reaffirmed their purpose rather than changing it by cursing the enemy with a prophecy that reiterated their purpose of dominion and authority over him: "And I will put enmity (open hostility) between you and the woman, and between your seed (offspring) and her Seed; He shall [fatally] bruise your head, and you shall [only] bruise His heel" (Genesis 3:15 AMP).

The serpent may have changed Adam and Eve's fate, but he did not change their purpose in God's plan. Inadvertently, in the process, he also sealed his own demise.

Because satan knows he still can't change our calling and purpose, he goes after our confidence instead. He follows us into our own hiding places and waits for us as he did in the garden and as those three girls waited for me. He charges at us and tries to hit us from the front while pulling us back from behind. He tries to kick us when we're down so that we never believe we can get up again. The enemy wants us to believe it's too hard or complicated to live out our purpose in this hustle culture, but that's just not the truth. God's purposes for us are not too hard to live out because Christ already did the work for us by fulfilling His purpose.

In the book of Hebrews, the writer spoke about the cross,

foreshadowed in Genesis, by pointing out that Jesus, the "author and finisher of our faith," not only endured the cross to take away the sin of the world, which began with Adam and Eve. He also endured and "despis[ed] the shame" that came with their sin, to free us from that too" (12:2 NKJV).

If we take a step back to see what the writer of Hebrews really meant when he said that Jesus "despised the shame," we see a picture that we sometimes gloss over when it comes to what Jesus truly endured for us.

Can you imagine being beaten to the point of being unrecognizable, stripped of all your clothes, and hung in front of everyone you knew? How would that make you feel?

The Greek word translated in English as *shame* is *aischuné*, which is used to describe shaming that is dishonoring, humiliating, and degrading.[4] By using this word, the writer wanted us to know that Jesus' death was not only painful and grotesque, but it was a deeply humiliating way to die.

In that moment our Lord felt the deep and overwhelming sense of embarrassment and guilt that humanity has carried since shame touched the story of creation. He endured it for the purpose of paying the price of any humiliation that would ever try to contaminate our lives. He carried it for our sin, our shame, and all the places we hide. He endured it for us.

Therefore, since the price for shame has already been paid through Jesus, we can come back to the original purposes of God's perfect plan, which came without shame.

He's calling us back to the place where we can build a life by design instead of default, but we have to be willing to answer His call.

Answering His Call

He's calling us back to the place where we can build a life by design instead of default, but we have to be willing to answer His call.

Just like all the people I called that night in my moment of despair, we have the choice to answer God's call or not. Sometimes we miss it, sometimes we ignore it, and other times we flat-out decline it, but it doesn't keep the call from coming through. On the other end of that call is an introduction to purpose that over time introduces us to a new language. I've learned the language that communicates surrender instead of striving, peace instead of force, and being instead of becoming. It's a language that articulates purpose apart from our achievements or accolades, and it's foreign to many of us because it's a language that is contrary to the primary language of our culture.

When we look around, we can see that we live in a culture that prides itself on external things. Our world places value on what is earned and achieved because measurable things offer a sense of perceived importance and power—but that is not the way of the kingdom, my friend. The world's toxic system of "doing" has contaminated the sacredness of what it truly means to answer the call of God. We are chasing our own tails, thinking that we need to do these great feats for the Lord to have worth, but that is a lie.

His calling is not a career or a landmark achievement, things the world has convinced us we need to live a life of meaning. No, the calling is simply allowing our feet to land and stand where our Father directs them in each season of life. It's listening to the still small voice that leads and guides us through a world that tries to convince us that our worth is found outside of who we already are in Christ.

Have you ever felt as if you needed to do more and wondered what God put you on this planet to do? Have you ever felt as if everyone around you is living life on a mission and you are still trying to figure out your own name? I want you to know that you are not the only one who feels like this. Part of the pitfall with purpose is that our road map toward our purpose as good citizens of this world often leaves us lost in perpetual detours, unsure which way to go. The map God gives His children looks radically different from the map the world presents to us. From an earthly standpoint, it's easy to set our gaze on what we can do instead of on Him who has already done it all for us. From a son or daughter's vantage point, our gaze is always watching where the Father is at work so we can respond to His leading rather than move on our own, with our fingers crossed that God will join us.

But how do we know where God is working?

This first place we see God working is in reconciliation with Him after being separated because of the fall of man. It's the pull of our hearts toward Him that restores the relationship between a holy God and those He created in His image and likeness. When we reconcile with God, it sets purpose back in our lives for us to accept rather than earn. We can hear God saying to us for the first time or the thousandth time, *I love you. I want you. I created you with a plan and a purpose. I'm with you.* The evidence of His affirmation is found in one of the most well-known Bible verses of all time. "For God so loved the world that He gave His only begotten Son, that whoever believes in Him should not perish but have everlasting life" (John 3:16 NKJV).

God gave Adam and Eve purpose in the garden, and He's giving purpose to you now. It's the same overall purpose we all have: to know Him and make Him known (John 17:3). In God's great mercy, He will continue to reignite this purpose in us because He desires for everyone to be saved and reconciled to Him and to come to the knowledge of truth so that we can discover the unique purpose and calling that's already in us (1 Timothy 2:4).

The other place we see God at work is in our commitment to move from accepting Jesus as our Savior to making Him the Lord of our life. It's the invitation to follow Him and allow ourselves to be molded and shaped into His image. This is the one where most people can see God at work in them, but they often choose to walk away as soon as they realize their response now impedes their comfort and convenience. I get it. I've walked away from God as a wife when it got too hard, as a mom when I lost too much control, and as a Christian when I felt suffocated by religious practices. I may have stopped moving toward my purpose when I walked away for a moment, but that didn't stop my purpose from calling to me every chance it got. When I found myself coming back to God and His purposes for my life, I realized I couldn't just say yes to Him; I needed to also say no to anything that tried to jack up my relationship with Him.

In the garden, this is the same place it got shady for Adam and Eve. They said yes to Paradise but no to paying the metaphorical mortgage to live there. They said yes to the promise but no to the stewardship of that promise. They said yes to the tree but no to watering its roots.

The hardest part about responding to God and His purposes is deciding to stop responding to anything else that would keep us from responding to Him. It's choosing to lend your ear to what He says rather than to what others say. It's being willing to believe that God wants to fellowship with you and spend time with you so He can show you that He's looking for you in love, not judgment. It's stepping out from behind the trees to let Him find you when you hear Him call, "Where are you?" (Genesis 3:9).

What part of your purpose has been hijacked because you couldn't commit to the inward and outward work it took to walk it out? How much time has passed since you last joined God where He is working to rediscover the passion and purpose you know still burn in your heart? Are you even close enough to see and hear God at work, or have you put His voice on silent and walked away?

Wherever you are, you're not too far. You're not out of earshot, and your purpose hasn't been cut off or silenced. But don't take my word for it. Here's the biblical truth you can rely on for yourself: "For the gifts and the calling of God are irrevocable" (Romans 11:29 NKJV).

Right now, God's purpose is calling you to remind you that He didn't change His number and He didn't change yours either. Stop ghosting Him, stop leaving His texts unread, and stop sending His calls to voicemail.

When we do take that brave step to reconcile with God and join where He's at work, the pieces come together. I saw God at work in those three girls who attacked me. I saw God at work in the relief I felt when someone finally answered my call. I saw God at work when I chose to respond to His purpose as I answered thousands upon thousands of calls, DMs, and texts from women who were bawling after an attack they never expected. It was the beginning of a beautiful merging of all my gifts and talents with His presence and plan. Like me, there are opportunities for you to merge with God that keep you in His presence instead of the world's pitfalls. And that will cause things to start changing.

The Pursuit of Purpose

Sometimes in our pursuit of purpose, we forget that shame can't come into the room until we become aware that we've done something wrong. The conundrum is that we're fallen, broken people so we can't help but do wrong. It's not an excuse; it's a reality. The Bible says it this way in the book of Romans: "For all have sinned and fall short of the glory of God" (3:23 NKJV).

None of us is perfect. Most of us are conscious of our failings and shortcomings.

Talk to a mom and she'll tell you she's far from perfect.

Talk to a dad and he'll tell you there is a list of things he would have done differently.

Talk to a spouse and they'll tell you a laundry list of areas they could improve.

Talk to a young person and they'll sheepishly withhold information to hide actions they can't undo.

Talk to an entrepreneur and they'll have advice on the dos and don'ts of business.

So then, if our humanity is too human to live without mistakes, how can we ever live without shame? How can we find freedom from a battle that we ourselves incite by our own flawed nature? How can we defeat an enemy that started talking to us at the beginning of creation and is still talking way too loud to us today?

Since day one, shame has been satan's weapon of choice to attack our pursuit of purpose. If unchecked and unaddressed, shame will paralyze us, making us ineffective in the kingdom and unable to bear fruit. I've been there.

As I shared previously, private poetry has been my language of coping and healing for as long as I can remember. I would pour my emotions onto pages and pages when I couldn't form words on my lips to convey the aches and woes of my spirit. Dark depression and deep brokenness penned some of the greatest monologues that my soul knew no one would ever hear. Tears of anguish would flood over rhythms that came from the deepest part of my being as a war cry for healing and change. I was committed to battling for something different from what my life depicted, and that war cry only got louder when I surrendered my life to Christ in 2015.

Through the prompting and leading of the Holy Spirit, my written words became spoken words of vulnerability. My spirit released all that shame had hidden from my past. I learned to trust the honest voice within me to speak boldly and brutally without abandon on the pages of my heart and beneath my pen. Still, my spoken words were for my private audience of One. I spoke out every word to God with the deep passion of a daughter who had finally come to accept her Father's unfailing love, and I sensed that passion turning into the small sparks of a fire.

I didn't know where or when God started to breathe on those sparks to create an all-consuming fire within me, but I do know that this inner fire was different. It enveloped my soul, but it didn't consume me the way the traumatizing experiences and painful memories it contained did. Every spoken word became a sacred personal statement of identity in God, and I found my purpose coming out of hiding with each utterance. God was giving me words that healed me, formed me, and released me from the shame that threatened to kill me. They were mine and mine alone. Sharing these poems with anyone was a vulnerability I wasn't ready to face.

I could hear God's calling getting louder and louder with each poem, but I ignored it and sent it to voicemail. Too many times to count, I'm pretty sure God thought, *This girl really thinks I'm going to stop calling.* He was right. I convinced myself God had called the wrong number anyway, so I just tuned it out and kept on moving and writing. Now, this was long before that horrible night at the young adult service where I forgot half the piece, so you already know God got His way, but I didn't know that, and I was pretty sure

God was giving me words that healed me, formed me, and released me from the shame that threatened to kill me.

43

I was going to win this battle to go public with God. I was wrong.

This was 2018, and I was hiding in the trees with my girl Eve, and we were having a great time acting as if we didn't hear God walking around looking for us.

"Where are you, Mariela?"

I thought, *He must be talking to someone else, because He of all people should know I'm way too naked in this garden of sin for Him to be looking for me. Truth be told, Eve is looking better than me with her one bite while I'm hiding in the dirt with all my pages and pages spilled over with poems of divorce, drugs, and drama. He's got to be talking to someone else.*

Have you ever ignored God so much that He sends someone else to be His microphone because He knows you can't send a whole, actual person to voicemail when she's sitting on your couch and refusing to leave? That's the story of She Speaks Fire.

So there I was, that horrible night when I forgot every word, having a conversation with a friend sitting on my couch who was telling me I had to get more of my spoken word out where people could find it. After humiliating myself, why would I want to speak *more*? Didn't she understand that my purpose had nothing to do with anyone else? As I was asking myself that very question, God asked me this:

Don't you understand that your purpose has everything to do with everyone else?

Umm, no. I was pretty sure I heard Him wrong. Tuning out His voice, I focused on convincing my friend *she* was wrong. That didn't work either. She wasn't on my side; she was definitely on God's side. So much so that she would not leave my house until I made a public Instagram on which to share all these private words—words I thought were just for me.

And just like that, She Speaks Fire was born, and I was terrified.

Who would ever want to hear what I had written?

Who would care what I had to say?

Who would believe anything I wrote could help them?

All the voices of shame came over me like a ton of bricks that I was sure would crush me if I even considered escaping the safety of my silence again. Louder than any spoken word I had ever written were the words of the enemy, taunting me to go back into hiding instead of answering God's invitation to accept His purpose for my life.

I had a choice. I could pick up the same ol' raggedy phone call that I've answered my whole life with shame's name scrawled across the caller ID, or I could pick up God's call to join Him at work. One was filled with a familiar lie, and one was filled with a new rhetoric of purpose. I chose to answer the latter.

Today, She Speaks Fire reaches hundreds of thousands daily with the purpose of setting other souls on fire for God while encouraging and equipping them to do the same for others. That's not me bragging about me. That's me bragging about Jesus and His faithfulness to the purpose within me that was greater than my shame and fear.

When I reflect on how God and His Garden Lessons have reclaimed my purpose, I can't help but remember the first spoken word I ever wrote. It was crafted from my honest heartache and rawest pain, and it paved the way to the richest of promises in God—a confirmation of my purpose and calling. When I read it today, I see how far I've come, how much soul work I've surrendered to, and how faithful God has been to me.

Who Am I?

I remember when I hated who I was
I was always searching but I could never find
That oh-so-desperate peace of mind
I searched and searched down countless paths
I was always searching but I could never have
Endless nights they were filled with tears
I tried to fit in for many years
Let me take it back to the beginning or as far
    as I can remember.
It was a cold, cold night. Let's just call it
    December.
I remember the day that we left my mom.
After that I didn't see her very much.

PURPOSE

It taught me to be distant and crave just any
    touch.
Because although my mother loved me,
and although my mother cared,
I needed her to nurture me
And I needed her to be there.
And so the quest for love ensued.
I would give, give, give and do, do, do.
Love me, love me
is what my soul kept screaming.
I was trapped inside of a prison.
My only escape was dreaming.
I turned to many things to fill the void.
The void that almost titled my life destroyed.
The void that would take but would never
    bring.
The void that consumed almost everything.
Actually, let me take that back,
because what it did bring was pain,
and what it did bring was shame,
and it made the void bigger.
Drugs. Sex. Cheating. Lying. Stealing.
I was unknowingly dying.
I was at the end of my rope.
I didn't care if I lived or if I died.
I was drowning in my sin.
But one day I came alive.

Jesus saved me.

He pulled me out of my misery.

He showered me with His love.

And now I'm truly living.

He showed me who I really am.

He took me off the treadmill

called approval of man

because in Him I stand

and I have my being.

He took the scales off my eyes

that were preventing me from seeing.

He showed me real love

when all I knew was rejection.

The kind of love that

doesn't require my participation.

You see, the kind of love that Jesus gives

is free from conditions.

I couldn't earn it. I couldn't buy it.

I could only accept it or I could deny it.

But even then, He remains faithful

because He can't deny who He is.

You see, He chose me

before the foundations of the world to be His.

He chose me.

A love so deep words cannot explain

but He chose me to carry His name.

He chose me.

PURPOSE

The liar, the cheater, the fornicator,
the girl with no hope
now has a relationship with her Creator.
He traded beauty for my ashes
and He made me alive.
He took away my fear
because in Him I live, and in Him I die.
So who am I?
I'm a daughter of a King.
I'm a light in darkness here to help set the
    captives free
because He lives in me.
And He's making His appeal to those who are
    dying,
to those who are hurting, to those who are crying
crying out to something more
to see, to be, to live, to soar
on the wings of an eagle
in the shadow of the Almighty,
to be led by green pastures and given rest.
So who am I? I am His.

I wrote that when I was at the peak of my identity crisis without any idea of who I was, what my voice was capable of, or how God would purpose it for His glory. All I knew was that God was asking me the same question again as I wrote each word: *Where are you, Mariela?*

Now I'm asking you the same question because, like mine, your answer may be what unlocks the courage in you to finally reclaim your purpose.

Daughter, where are you?

Mama, where are you?

Sister, where are you?

Wife, where are you?

Friend, where are you?

Boss babe, where are you?

Artist, where are you?

Lawyer, where are you?

Entrepreneur, where are you?

Leader, where are you?

Teacher, where are you?

[Insert whatever title you or the world has given you], where are you?

It's time to come out from the dirt and let what God has been doing in private come into the light. And when you do, you'll find your voice of purpose will speak the fire within you.

Garden Reflection

In this conversation about purpose, where are you?

- Where are you with your purpose? Are you hiding from it or living with passion and pursuit? Is this where you want to be, or have pitfalls taken you on a detour?

- Where are you with your relationships with others? Is this where you want to be?
- Where are you with God, and how did you get there? Is this where you want to be?

If you're not at a reconciled place with God, can I lead you through a prayer of surrender?

Father, You know all the places I've been hiding and all the places in my life where I've walked away. I'm tired of running and tired of being lost. I need You in my life as my Lord and Savior. I believe You died on the cross and rose the third day so that I would have a road paved for me to be reconciled with You. I know I have sinned against You, and I'm here before You, without any fig leaves, asking for Your forgiveness. Please come near to me so that I may know You and the plans You have for my life. I surrender all I am to You, and I commit to walk out this journey with You starting today. I believe in You and trust You with all my heart. In Jesus' name, amen.

SPEAKING FIRE INTO YOUR PURPOSE

I declare that my purpose is secure in Christ because I am confident that God has great plans for me, and I am filled with hope for a great future [Jeremiah 29:11]. I believe and receive the truth that He who has begun a good work in me will complete it [Philippians 1:6].

GARDEN
LESSON
Three

Community

From Hurting to Whole

I never thought I would be the girl in an abusive relationship. In my ignorance I quietly judged women who tolerated abuse as though breaking free from it were as simple as dotting the i's or crossing the t's; but there I was, unable to dot said *i* or cross said *t*.

At twenty-six I was divorced from my husband and in an extremely emotionally abusive relationship with a guy I didn't know how to get away from. My entire world revolved around him, my mind was consumed with thoughts of him, and I had lost myself trying to please him.

Before this relationship I had been married, but after the birth of our first child, my husband and I went through a rough patch in our marriage. We didn't know the Lord at the time and were living fast lives filled with a lot of chaos and wild living. I was young, vulnerable, and extremely broken when I had our first daughter. I carried a deep well of shame inside me and an incessant need to find anything that could potentially fill the void. My husband filled that void for a while, but when we started butting heads, I searched elsewhere. I had been working a corporate job since a year after our daughter was born, and a male coworker started paying me a lot of attention. He was charming, funny, and very aware that I was married.

He would make jokes with a flirtatious tone but made a point to say, "But you're married," as though the statement would keep the original intention of what he had said at bay. He started asking questions about my husband and disparaging him and telling me that I deserved better while simultaneously pumping himself up to be the perfect guy.

After months of entertaining inappropriate conversations and a level of emotional intimacy that should have been reserved for only my husband, I mentally checked out of my marriage. I spent my time daydreaming about a life with my coworker and dreading the life I had at home because the attention made me feel seen and desired. The moment my husband did something that justified my desire for a divorce, I asked for one. He didn't object because he knew

I had already divorced him in my mind and heart. All that was left to do was sign the paperwork.

The emotional affair with my coworker became a full-blown relationship that lasted close to three years, but those were three of the loneliest years of my life. This man broke me down mentally and convinced me that I could not live without him. I was so dependent on him that I would put his needs before my own and endure cruel treatment for the little crumbs of love he would give me when he saw fit. Not only was I neglecting myself and my own needs; I was also neglecting the nurturing, intimate relationship I'd once had with my daughter. Her physical needs were met, but she wasn't my priority. The disconnect between us was more painful than any disconnect I had with myself, and the rift multiplied the deep sorrow and guilt I carried.

Even though the relationship with my coworker brought so much anguish and shame into my life, I stayed because my worth was attached to his every word. The overarching theme of our relationship was secrecy, as I was not allowed to visit his home or his family, which drove me into more and more shame. He wasn't married, but he wanted a separate life away from me whenever he was tired of me.

I wanted out of the relationship, but I didn't know how to get out. I felt dead inside. However, being dead puts you in the perfect position to meet the One who has the power to resurrect dead things.

While abuse and shame lurked around every part of

my heart, the love of the Father pursued me in the most uncommon way. God used two ordinary women from my daughter's after-school program to bear witness of His love. Week after week I observed and was intrigued by the joy they carried and their resilience to my constant rejection of church invites. I noticed they were not deterred by my objections or snarky remarks about Christians and how judgmental they were. Their consistency in character spoke volumes to me and laid the foundation for the work God was starting to do in my life as an adult. I wasn't saved at the time, and these women were slowly bringing me into community with them and with their God.

One day I walked in to pick up my daughter and was feeling extremely depressed. Despite not being in the mood to talk, something prompted me to linger. There was a cream-colored couch in front of Mrs. Deanna's desk that drew me in as if I were on the losing end of a tug-of-war match. I didn't know why I wanted to stay, but I now know I was finally ready to be seen for real. The other teacher, Jasmine, asked, "Mariela, are you okay?" And I began to weep uncontrollably.

Mrs. Deanna hugged me and whispered in my ear, "Jesus said, 'Come to Me, all who are weary and carry heavy burdens. My yoke is easy and My burden is light.'"

I had no idea she was referencing Matthew 11:28 or what it meant, but that was the first time I allowed myself to really be seen at my worst, and I felt no shame. Before I left, Jasmine recommended I listen to "Why I Hate Religion but Love Jesus" by Jefferson Bethke and told me his book *Jesus > Religion* helped her see Jesus in a new way. I didn't think much of it because I wasn't much of a reader back then, but before I could object, she blurted out, "Here! Take my Audible password and listen to it. I am not much of a reader, but listening to books helps me a lot." It was as though she were in my mind. I now know it was God, but I was tripping in that moment. I downloaded the Audible app and started listening right away. Bethke's book opened my eyes to a God who was both familiar and different from the God my daddy had introduced me to as a little girl. I still didn't know God, but I was intrigued to learn more.

I thought the "more" that I was looking for would come exclusively from God, but I had it all wrong. The "more" I needed would come just as it came through Mrs. Deanna— in community.

The Not Good, the Good, and the Ugly

Community was introduced first in the garden, and we can see from the start that it was a good thing: "Then the LORD God said, 'It is not good for the man to be alone. I will make a helper who is just right for him'" (Genesis 2:18 NLT).

Adam was in the middle of Paradise and in the presence of God, surrounded by every resource he could ever need or want, but God shook His head and said, "No, something is missing."

Adam was set! Think about it—he had full access to God and the freedom to create without limitation or hindrance. If Adam were alive today, every guru on the internet would tell him to hunker down and build an empire for himself, but no, God said Adam needed someone—his "person"—to come alongside him to help him fulfill his assignment.

Have you ever heard someone say, "I don't need people; I just need God"? Maybe you've said it. But while the sentiment is understandable and even admirable, it's erroneous. Don't get me wrong; I was once the person who devoted herself to being alone with God in prayer, in worship, and away from the world. I even got a little self-righteous and stuck my nose up at those who didn't carry the same devotion, as though I was *so* committed—but I learned the hard way that a life with God alone isn't enough.

That's a scandalous statement, isn't it?

Before you throw your stones, hear me out.

It's not me saying that God alone isn't enough; God Himself said it when He said it wasn't good for Adam to be alone.

In the perfect world He created, God designed His creation not only to be dependent on Him but to need each other. Adam needed more than God to fulfill his mission. He needed Eve.

According to *Smith's Bible Dictionary*, the word *man*

in Genesis 2:18 is translated from the generic Hebrew term for the human race.[5] One can read that scripture and think God was only talking about that first male human, but His statement actually applies to all human beings. God was saying it's not good for man, woman, boy, or girl to be alone. Fast-forward beyond Genesis and we still see the garden principles of community in motion. We see community when the psalmist wrote, "God sets the lonely in families" (Psalm 68:6). We see community when Jesus called the disciples into community with Him in the New Testament. And we see community modeled again when Jesus returned from the solace of prayer to rejoin the disciples whom He knew would carry on the importance of community long after He was crucified. Each example brings us back to the beginning, to the garden, and to God's heart for community.

Before sin entered the world, Adam and Eve were naked and unashamed and in community with God. They shared the innocence of God's creative genius that allowed them to be fully seen and fully known by each other. It wasn't just their bodies that were naked; it was their whole being. Their gifts, their personalities, and their raw thoughts were without covering. They were shame-free.

When sin entered the world, shame replaced innocence with isolation and hidden judgment. We see this in Adam and Eve covering themselves from each other and thereby breaking the pure bond of genuine community, which made them vulnerable to the enemy.

Satan banks on the fact that it's downright crippling to try to do life on our own. He delights in our decision to retreat from relationships and partnerships because he knows it's only a matter of time before we find ourselves drowning with our arms flailing in desperation for a hand to reach out and save us. He cheers in victory when we stand in isolation because he revels in our neglect of community. This is why the author of Hebrews reminded us, "Give attentive, continuous care to watching over one another, . . . not forsaking or neglecting to assemble together [as believers], as is the habit of some people, but admonishing (warning, urging, and encouraging) one another, and all the more faithfully as you see the day approaching" (10:24–25 AMPC).

Now, you might be thinking, *I've done life on my own all this time, and I'm doing just fine. I'm not forsaking or neglecting community. I just don't need it.* But let me remind you again what God said in Genesis: it isn't good to be alone.

We may be able to accomplish incredible feats on our own, but is that *good*?

Is it good to get to the end of our finish line and have no one to share the triumph with?

Is it good to accomplish a dream or goal but be too exhausted from doing it alone to enjoy it?

Is it good to do it all alone just because you can?

You may reflect on your life and feel as though your life is all good, but is it good that you're in this alone? I would ask, *Why* are you doing it alone? Is it because you've encountered one too many toxic people with hidden agendas and motives, who take more than they give? Or is it because you don't want people to see the part of *you* that is toxic? For most of us, it's probably a combination of both that leads us away from community.

Sis, shame loves to sell us on the idea that the toxic and dysfunctional parts of ourselves need to be addressed in secrecy and in isolation before we can come into community so we can avoid the risk of rejection and judgment, but that's a straight-up lie. We don't experience healing and wholeness in isolation; we heal in the openness of community. I think of Lazarus when Jesus resurrected him from the grave but then called him out into the openness of community so that those around him could aid in his being healed completely: "Jesus called in a loud voice, 'Lazarus, come out!' The dead man came out, his hands and feet wrapped with strips of linen, and a cloth around his face. Jesus said to them, 'Take off the grave clothes and let him go'" (John 11:43–44).

We don't experience healing and wholeness in isolation; we heal in the openness of community.

But what if your wounds and graveclothes came from a fragmented and toxic community in your past? Too many of us have been born or placed into family, social, or religious communities that have left us broken, bruised, and battered. But in Christ and in community we discover together that the nakedness of our wounds is covered by the God who is perfect in every way. Yes, people may have done real damage in our lives, but there are other people God can use to bring real healing as well. We miss the beauty of the body of Christ when we assume the toxicity of one community will also be part of the next community to which God brings us. Just as in a human body, the body heals the body. Everything the body needs to regenerate new life is within the body, and healing can happen naturally if given time and opportunity. The body of Christ works similarly. The cells of our fellowship, the breath in our worship, and the new language of our renewed minds all work together with the Holy Spirit to bring healing as only the body of Christ can if given time and opportunity.

Maybe your experience with the body of Christ was different from what I just described. It doesn't mean you need to leave community; it means you need to come back to the original design for community that Paul described to the church of Corinth when they, too, questioned the need for community in the church.

In fact, some parts of the body that seem weakest and least important are actually the most necessary. And the parts we regard as less honorable are those we clothe with the greatest care. So we carefully protect those parts that should not be seen, while the more honorable parts do not require this special care. So God has put the body together such that extra honor and care are given to those parts that have less dignity. This makes for harmony among the members, so that all the members care for each other. If one part suffers, all the parts suffer with it, and if one part is honored, all the parts are glad. (1 Corinthians 12:22–26 NLT)

The enemy will try to convince you that you need to hide yourself instead of coming into community to find healing, and he usually uses the fear of rejection and judgment to do it—but he is playing us!

He's going to tell you that you're better off alone.

He's going to tell you that you're just going to get hurt again, so why try?

He's going to tell you that you're safest when you're out of community, not in it.

He's going to tell you lies on top of lies, and all three of the previous statements are just that.

What he won't tell you is this:

When all hope is lost and you need a reminder of who you are—isolation won't deliver.

When your heart feels like it is being torn out of your chest because of an unexpected tragedy or loss— isolation won't sit with you as you weep.

When you are losing faith, and doubt is consuming
your mind—isolation won't speak the truth but
will further feed the lie.

The truth is that community—not isolation—has always
been a part of God's redemptive plan for our lives. He draws
us in with His loving-kindness but keeps us through His
chosen instruments, which come in the form of people. It's
people who will encourage you and exhort you in the faith,
so your heart doesn't become hardened through the deceit-
fulness of sin (Hebrews 3:13).

It's in community that we find restoration for our truest selves, which were made in the image of the Father, the
Son, and the Holy Spirit. Going back to the garden story in
the beginning chapter of Genesis, we read that God created
humanity in "our" image (1:26). Many Christian traditions
read this "our" as referring to the Son and the Holy Spirit.
According to this theological interpretation, creation was
birthed *in* community, *for* community, and *with* community because that's the image God modeled from Genesis to
Revelation.

In His image, we are whole individually and collectively
as He is whole individually and collectively with Jesus and
the Holy Spirit. When we can live our lives in tandem with
others, we take the Garden Lesson of community and find
the courage to live authentically with others and without
fear or shame.

Hiders, Runners, Fighters, and Skeptics

The body of Christ isn't perfect. We will oftentimes openly confess our need for God but fumble when expressing our need for others. We know we need people, and we know we want people, but we tend to want people on *our* terms and based on *our* boundaries. It sounds like this:

> *I'll roll with you as long as you only see me walk and run but never crawl.*
> *We can succeed together in ministry, but I don't want to be so connected that if something goes wrong, we experience communal shame together.*
> *You can be part of my today, but there's no guarantee you'll be part of my tomorrow.*
> *I'll let you follow me from a distance, but you can't follow me up close and personal.*

We desperately want to believe these terms and conditions can insulate us, but the church is no different from the garden in Genesis. Sometimes things just slither in. If anything has the power to divide and disgrace a community, it's shame. It can separate us from others because—let's face it: no one wants people all up in your business when your business isn't doing well. It's daunting and terrifying to let people in your community see the real you without the filters and facades.

But real life doesn't have filters and facades, and we live in the real world.

Online platforms can feel like the real world because they're run by real people, but they're not reality. They can seem real and they can replicate real, but we've got to be able to see them for what they are, not what they appear to be.

Take, for example, social platforms. These online communities have a premise for performance, so it's not a surprise that we label our online presence as a platform. It's so easy to pose, perform, and position ourselves to gain likes and follows for an audience we only see and hear from a distance. In-person communities make it much more difficult to carry a fake persona, but it's almost comical how quickly we can hide our true identities behind a digital profile.

Can we tell the difference between who people are on our digital screens and who they are in person?

Every one of us needs to have a community that supports one another individually and collectively so we see and experience the healthiness that comes from authentic relationship. The hardest part about that statement is that people are people, and in community, people can be both the problem and the solution.

As imperfect people, we have control issues, insecurity issues, rejection issues, anger issues, and myriad other issues that would take up more pages than I could write in a lifetime. I've got issues; you've got issues; we've all got issues.

So what the heck does a healthy community look like if we've all got issues?

For my hiders, community looks like a group of people you can just be real with. Breathe with. A group can be just two people instead of two hundred people. The number of people isn't important; the number of times you're honest with these people is. For you, community is more about the transparency of your relationships than the quantity of your relationships.

So what the heck does a healthy community look like if we've all got issues?

For my runners, community can be the people who hold on to you when you're ready to jet. These are the folks who can speak the truth in love because you aren't questioning if they genuinely love you. You know they've got your back, so you aren't afraid to let them see you. For you, community is defined by honesty and accountability and expressed in security.

For my fighters, community is found in those who can weather your ups and downs and steady your ship. Relationships that you give permission to bring peace to your chaos are the ones that cause the wars within you to cease. These are the relationships that ground you in why your peace is more important than your fight. For you, community is where you can put down your metaphorical guns and knives—like angry words, resentful attitudes, and aggressive opinions—without the fear that those around you won't put down theirs.

For my skeptics, community comes from the people who can see and speak into your thought closet while helping you live in both truth and faith. These are the folks who can instill faith into your fears, hope into your doubts, and truth into your lies. For you, community is where you are free to be among those who value and treasure the marriage of what you see with your eyes and what you believe in your heart.

Can you find yourself in one of those? Does your current community look and sound like the kind of community you need based on where you are today? Can you be honest enough to say there's a little bit of a hider, a runner, a fighter, and a skeptic in you?

Regardless of who you are, we need you in our community as the body of Christ. Yup, we need the hider, the runner, the fighter, the skeptic, and all other parts of you that you don't want anyone to see. When a hider finds a fighter, she finds someone who will fight to keep her out of the darkness of isolation. When a runner finds a skeptic, he discovers a relationship that can bring him into maturity and longevity by the truths he's not afraid to confront. We need the imperfect parts of one another to push, challenge, and unlock the best in us.

I know that's the kind of community I want to be part of, but I also know this kind of godly community isn't always easy to find.

Holy Places of Hurt

Ideally, the church should be the one place where we can live authentically, without fear, as a community, but as I already mentioned, that's not some people's experience. Just as Jesus experienced before His crucifixion, the deepest bruises and bloodiest beatings often come at the hands of church people, not sinners.

Let me stop before anyone gets it twisted. I can tell you that I fundamentally, wholeheartedly, and unapologetically love God's house. Not one part of me is a church hater or a church skeptic. I believe in, trust, and need the holiness and sanctity the church represents as the bride of Christ, and I'm here for it all day, every day—not just on Sundays.

But I'd be lying if I told you the church hasn't sometimes looked more like the enemy of Christ than the bride of Christ. And my purpose in talking openly about a typically swept-under-the-rug conversation is not to bash or hurt the church but to follow the model of the garden. "Then God said to the man, 'I commanded you not to eat from that tree. But you listened to your wife and ate from it. So I will curse the ground because of you. You will have to work hard all your life for the food the ground produces'" (Genesis 3:17 ERV).

When Adam and Eve sinned, God didn't curse *them*; He cursed the *ground*. After He exposed their sin, He told Adam that because of his sin, he would have to work harder, against thorns and thistles. When sin comes into our communities of worship today, God doesn't curse *us*; He exposes our sins and tells us we're going to have to get to work too, and we, too, will have "thorny" issues to face. God didn't shy away from exposing the sin in the first community, and I'm here for a real, honest conversation about sin in our communities as well.

Power, position, and authority can make people do crazy things, say crazy things, and act in crazy ways and end up victimizing people worse than the world can outside the church walls. People *expect* blows of manipulation, abuse, and neglect from the world, but they don't expect them in the name of their God. It changes something in the minds and hearts of believers when they experience their deepest pain in the house of God. It's not just church hurt they must deal with; it's a spiritual violation of the sacred relationship between the Father and His kids. Faith is the very fabric of the church, and when people are broken and bleeding at the hands of people they'd expected to trust, asking them to trust again in a faith community can be nearly impossible.

A few years after starting She Speaks Fire, I shared coffee with a woman who was so deeply traumatized by church hurt that she vowed never to be part of a church community again. Let's call her Ingrid. As she shared her shame story, she repeated a saying I had heard before but didn't fully understand until that moment: church hurt is the worst hurt.

I listened quietly as she shared how she had been a leader at a church for almost fifteen years before she found out a shameful truth about her pastor. The so-called shepherd she was following showed himself to be a wolf. For over ten years he had been having an affair with a young woman in their church. It resulted in pregnancy. As Ingrid's story unraveled in front of me, she wrestled with the incredulous detail that other people knew and suspected over the course of the past decade, but they were too afraid to speak. To some, her pastor was a benevolent and compassionate leader, and to others he was a tyrannical monster. To Ingrid, he was the former, and seeing him as a wolf brought an onslaught of anger, confusion, disappointment, and sadness. In the moment of his exposure, she looked around and wondered if others were real or just more wolves in disguise. If it was possible for the shepherd of the house to abuse those entrusted to his care, she wondered who could really be trusted in that place.

When spiritual abuse like this man's is exposed in a church, everyone is exposed. This wasn't just a man to Ingrid; he was her trusted and beloved pastor, mentor, and father figure. When he fell publicly, she, along with thousands of others, felt the rocking and shaking of the house. He was removed from all levels of leadership, and while Ingrid agreed with the removal, she was unprepared for the shame, panic, rage, and frailty that came as a result. One Sunday she was taking notes from his preaching from the pulpit, and the next he and his pregnant victim were gone from sight and all conversations. Hers was a story of abandonment and betrayal all wrapped up in one messy chapter in her church's history.

At the end of her story, she told me she couldn't go back to church because she didn't believe it was even possible to survive as a church community after such a loss and betrayal. The sin wasn't hers, but she felt the shame of association as a member of his church.

Did she weep for a man she had put her faith in? *Yes.*

Did she despise him for the choices he had made that painfully brought shame to everyone connected to him? *Yes.*

Did she want him back and at the same time want him to stay away? *Yes.*

Did she hurt and turn against fellow congregants because his decisions had forced them all to make decisions on what would happen next to their community? *Yes.*

Did she have to hold the pieces of her own heart while healing the hearts of those around her? *Yes.*

Did she believe the end of his story as her pastor translated to the end of her in that community? *Yes.*

Was she wrong? *Yes.*

I gave her a tissue and wiped my own tears away. Then I reminded her that God removes people and things in a church community because it's what's best for the church as a whole, not the church as individuals. His vantage point from heaven gives God a wider perspective to help communities make the difficult decisions to expose church hurts before those hurts become church culture. There was peace for Ingrid instead of shame when she accepted that her pastor had to be removed because the culture he had begun to value was not that of the kingdom. Yes, she hurt in the process, but I encouraged her to go back to God's house so that a grace to heal, a grace to be truly seen, and a grace to be truly loved by God could be birthed from their communal pain.

If you've been part of a church community like Ingrid's that has known the bloodshed and pain of spiritual manipulation, abuse, or neglect, I need you to know it may have changed you, but it didn't change God. It didn't change the fact that His house is still the body of Christ where people come to experience a one-on-one encounter with the real God of redemption and grace.

I can tell you this with full confidence and authority because sin and shame in the garden may have changed Adam and Eve, but it didn't change God. The first sin didn't change the fact that God still, millennia later, wants His sons and daughters to come back to His Son to experience a one-on-one encounter with a real Savior who could silence their shame once and for all.

Just because you or I had an encounter with one of His sheep who went astray doesn't mean God went astray too. He didn't fail you and He didn't forsake you. Your purpose didn't change because your community got shaken or torn down. You're going to heal and you're going to move forward. Maybe not today and maybe not tomorrow, but you will heal.

Your community needs you to heal because they need

you. We need *you*. We don't need you because of what you do or what titles you carry; we need you because our communities can exist in health only when we choose to fight for interdependence instead of conforming to isolation. That is, when we see the value in ourselves, the value in one another, and the value in who we are together.

Close your eyes and see yourself being seen and known within an authentic community.

See your community strong and healthy.

Envision being part of a community that reflects genuine interdependence instead of isolation.

Imagine a community of people who know that nakedness of soul and spirit is a gift, not a punishment or a curse.

Let yourself have faith again in a community that is healed and actively working to heal from past hurts and traumas.

Now, open your eyes, wipe your tears, and go build it.

Garden Prayer

Father, You know the pain and longing of my heart for genuine godly community. You walk with me when I have no community, broken community, and whole community. You have seen the parts of me that hide, run, fight, and question in skepticism. I'm thankful that these places in me don't surprise You or remove me from community with You.

Help me rebuild community again the same way You rebuilt community after the fall with Adam and Eve. I release every place of shame that has created walls of isolation and ask that You show me how to keep releasing shame to You as I move through these Garden Lessons. I surrender all my hurts to You because I know You can make me whole.

For all the healing You have done so far and for all You have yet to do in me, I thank You. Make my heart ready so that the community You see is the community I build. In Jesus' name I pray, amen.

SPEAKING FIRE INTO YOUR COMMUNITY

I declare that isolation and fear will not lead me away from the gift of community [Isaiah 41:10]. Even in my hurt, I will not doubt the Lord's ability to heal [Psalm 69:20]. I choose today to rejoice with the truth and always protect, always trust, always hope, always persevere [1 Corinthians 13:6–7].

Approval

Approval Addiction

After I got saved, I became deeply involved in a local church and fell in love with serving and being "used by God." I started leading a small group, upward of twenty-five women who would show up at my house every Thursday night, eager and ready to hear what the Lord wanted to say to each of them. I took pride in the number of women who came and allowed me to disciple them each week. I was celebrated for what I was doing, but no one noticed that my heart wasn't right. Don't get me wrong; I love discipling women, pouring into them, and giving everything

I can to them. But for a while, I was doing it from the wrong place.

Remember that little girl who threw a birthday party that no one came to? Well, she grew up, and even though she learned how to pretend with the best of them, she was still always afraid she'd end up sitting alone at a table again. That little girl inside me was constantly telling grown-up me that I needed to do whatever it took to be the kind of woman people wanted to celebrate, befriend, and be around. No matter what it cost me or who I had to become, I was desperate to be a small group leader who was surrounded by people who loved and praised her. I was obsessed with being someone everyone approved of and never again disappointed by people because of abandonment or rejection. I still believed the lie shame told, that I had to earn love instead of merely being worthy of it because I was alive.

I knew I had a problem and I remember the anxiety and near panic that raced through me when people didn't show up. I was addicted to the approval I received from these women and the affirming nod of my pastor when he saw me sitting with all my disciples in the congregation. Ignoring the nagging, familiar feeling of addiction, I focused on how great I felt with all the approval and validation I was getting. Addiction was a drug-and-alcohol thing, not a God thing, so it couldn't be the same. How could a right result come from the wrong place?

I didn't know it was possible to value the validation and

attention of people in such a dysfunctional way that I could become addicted to the approval of man and crave it as a junkie does her next fix. I was a people pleaser through and through, and with every affirming nod, smile, or compliment, my shame was silenced a little bit more because I felt a temporary sense of the love I craved so badly—even if it was fake and manufactured by my own doing.

I was "killin' it," as my pastor would say, but no one was paying attention that I was also killin' my marriage. I was raised in the church era when "power couple" was the thing and something every couple was striving to be. I was under immense pressure from our church, our leaders, and our pastors to serve and do it all in the name of God, but the truth was, I was doing it all from an unhealthy place. My husband and I would go to church, and we would be bombarded by the pressure to start another group—a marriage group, because we were this "power couple." My husband was not about it, so I would pressure him and hold resentment when he wouldn't agree to do more. I was mad that he didn't want to start a marriage group on another night in our home. I was irritated that he didn't want to serve in the church every Sunday. I was frustrated that he didn't want to please everyone as I did. Secretly, of course.

My need for approval and validation led to my grossly devaluing my marriage and questioning if God had really restored this man of mine. If God had restored him, why wasn't he performing the way I thought he should?

We fought for years, yet still showed up with fake smiles on our faces every Sunday. It wasn't until God made some drastic changes in our church that I saw we were operating from a very unhealthy culture of demand and serving, even to the detriment of our own families, for the sake of growth. And I was one of the first to show up, drink the Kool-Aid, and ask for a big ol' refill. Instead of taking time to grow in our personal relationship and establish healthy changes, I wanted him to get to work publicly. I had traded my purpose and identity in God for the purpose and identity I found in the approval and validation of my pastors and church leaders. I knew God was talking to me about it all, but I wasn't ready to hear it. I just wanted to show up and live in the glory of the numbers and stay numb to the truth of what I was neglecting, and because of that, a new addiction creeped into my life. I had traded my drug addiction for approval addiction, and no one knew.

I carried so much shame when I walked into the house of God, though that should have been the place where I felt the most refreshed and encouraged. Eventually my approval addiction drove my husband to decide not to go to church anymore because of the pressure from other church folks and the pressure from me at home. I felt like a failure, embarrassed that we were no longer going to be seen as the "power couple" who could do it all. I had shame in my spirit, embarrassment on my face, a hard heart for my husband, and a lie in my mouth that everything was just fine. Different drug, same bondage.

I'm thankful Justin didn't allow me or anyone else to bully him into doing something for approval or being someone he wasn't for the sake of validation. I'm grateful I found peace with myself and my relationship with God because it gave me the courage to face my own addiction. Human approval almost took me out, but God used it to bring me back to a place of honesty before Him so I could live honest before others. For that and so much more, I give glory to God.

Today, I stand firmly on Galatians 1:10: "Am I now trying to win the approval of human beings, or of God? Or am I trying to please people? If I were still trying to please people, I would not be a servant of Christ."

It's crazy to think about how shame works, because in the same way that diets seem to convince us that all food is bad, shame will tell us all approval is good. And like the failure of extreme dieting, extreme perspectives about approval don't work either. We are born needing approval, and it's okay to admit it. From infancy to adulthood, we all want to hear that what we're doing and who we are is seen, recognized, and appreciated. We, as humans, ache to be affirmed for our very existence as well as our efforts, and there's no shame in that. Our need is not the problem. The problem lies in where we seek affirmation and why we're willing to pawn ourselves, our purpose, and sometimes our convictions to get it.

Already Enough

When we grow up thinking we must constantly *be* something to be approved or affirmed, we never quite find that place of fulfillment and rest in who we already *are* and in what God has already *done*. Life becomes a series of actions to show off and toot our own horns rather than a series of actions that show off what God has done and is still doing in our lives. We focus on all the things we still need to do to be able to say we've arrived instead of being able to look at what Christ already did on the cross when we did absolutely nothing. Romans 5:8 shows us that He didn't die a brutal death on the cross out of punishment for how *bad* we were but to demonstrate how *loved* we are by Him: "But God demonstrates his own love for us in this: While we were still sinners, Christ died for us."

If that doesn't get you to fully believe in God's approval and affirmation of you, let's go back to the garden. Before sin and shame had even come onto the scene and before Adam and Eve had ever done a thing, God had already approved and affirmed humanity. The Bible says, "And God saw everything that he had made, and behold, it was very good" (Genesis 1:31 ESV).

Did you read that? He looked, He saw, and He called it *very* good. He wasn't just looking at a compromised version of His creation and tolerating it. No, He was pleased with it and made sure to express and publicly approve and affirm how very good it was. In fact, after He made each part of creation, He "saw that it was good." He didn't just declare our goodness in His sight once, and He didn't just say it after He was done. He acknowledged goodness as He formed every part of creation.

Why are His approval and affirmation of our goodness throughout the process of creation so good for us to know? When we encounter them at each part of the creation process, we learn something special about God: He delights in the process of creating and has no hesitation in declaring His approval every step of the way. This means we can find His approval and affirmation in our own process of healing and self-discovery rather than looking for it only at the end. The world we live in tells us we have to get to the finish line before we can have a shot at the medal, but God modeled through the creation story that He works differently.

Light: "And God saw the light, that it was good" (Genesis 1:4 NKJV).

Dry land and seas: "And God saw that it was good" (Genesis 1:10 ESV).

Vegetation: "And God saw that it was good" (Genesis 1:12 ESV).

Sun, moon, and stars: "And God saw that it was good" (Genesis 1:18 ESV).

Sea creatures and birds: "And God saw that it was good" (Genesis 1:21 ESV).

Land creatures: "And God saw that it was good"
(Genesis 1:25 ESV).
All of creation: "And God saw everything that he had
made, and behold, it was very good" (Genesis
1:31 ESV).

God isn't emotionally neglectful and understands our
need for approval and affirmation, which is why I believe He
has been so vocal about it from the beginning. He isn't keeping us guessing on where He stands and where we stand in
relation to Him. In the New Testament the Father's approval
was beautifully displayed at the baptism of Jesus when the
sky opened and "a voice from heaven said, 'This is my Son,
whom I love; with him I am well pleased'" (Matthew 3:17).

You know what I love most about this public display
of approval? I love that Jesus hadn't performed one miracle
or even started His life of ministry when this was spoken
over Him. Adam and Eve had not done anything either
before God called them good. Do you see the pattern here?
God's approval is based on who we *are*, not what we *do*. In

God's approval is based on who we *are*, not what we *do*.

Christ we are sons and daughters
of God, and His approval of us is
not fickle like the world's; it doesn't
change because He doesn't change
(Hebrews 13:8).

Friend, God is saying to you
today: *You are My daughter, whom*

I love, and with you I am well pleased. Or *Son, you have My approval, and I love you just because you're My child.* Allow that truth to sink down deep inside you and own it. Live from that place and build your house on the steady consistency of the Father's approval of you.

Listen to me: shame ain't loyal to you. So you have no reason to stay loyal to it. What do I mean? Shame's priority is not you, your family, your purpose, or your future. Its priority is keeping you close so that it can have authority and influence over you. It has no vested interest in your freedom, only your bondage. It's not moved with emotion when it watches you destroy your life. It carries no remorse for the havoc it wreaks. Shame is not your friend, and you don't have to keep inviting it into your heart. It doesn't deserve your trust. God does.

It's time to fully believe you and I are already enough so the disapproval of people cannot hurt us any longer, nor can their approval or affirmation ever trump the approval and affirmation God has already declared over us. We can finally stop chasing after the dangling carrot.

Jesus Himself warned us not to practice our righteousness to be seen by others. At the beginning of Matthew 6, He mentioned giving to the needy, praying, and fasting as things we ought to practice in secret, reiterating the value of God's approval over man's (vv. 1–4). He went as far as to say there is no reward from our Father in heaven when we do these things for the approval of others (v. 1). Over and over in this biblical chapter, God reminds us that our heavenly Father sees all that we do—whether others do or not. But verse 33 tells us amid all of our "doing" to "seek first the kingdom of God and his righteousness" (NKJV). Then and only then will He reward us for our efforts: "And all these things shall be added to you." His words are the ultimate assurance that we can look to Him for approval and affirmation and that they will last longer than any attention or applause from others.

If we don't surrender our approval addiction to God's Word, you and I will always perform for the next standing ovation, the next stamp of validation, and the next follow, like, or share on social media.

The Tech Trap of Shame

For an approval addict, our technological and digital age can make taking our eyes off the dangling carrots even trickier. Social media offers immediate approval and affirmation through clicks, likes, views, shares, and follows. For those of us who are addicted to the applause of others, it's a slippery slope of temporary praise and perpetual torment all at the same time. Our screens might offer relief any time we scroll, but the immediate gratification of the digital world capitalizes on the temptation to seek approval and affirmation in unhealthy ways.

Social media has become the new, modern-day fruit that promises to open our eyes to good and evil, but it's the same old trap. It promises something it can deliver only for a fleeting moment. And after the chewing stops and we've swallowed the lie in one big, shameful gulp, we can't help but look down at our sinful, imperfect selves and see the flaws glaringly apparent.

I remember talking to another social media influencer who shared with me how belittled she felt in her insecurities. She didn't feel complete or good about herself, so she would sew together some fig leaves in the form of an Instagram story or post to try to convince people she didn't see or even know that she was doing great and still worthy of their follow. She confessed through tears that she secretly counted hand claps, likes, and comments to fill her inner value meter. And when she didn't get the applause she craved, she sat in digital silence, feeling worse about herself, and the cycle of digital approval addiction continued.

Without a dependence on God that goes down deep, those of us dealing with suppressed unworthiness end up wounded because we tried to gain a sense of worth and validation from other people instead of resting in the approval and affirmation of who God says we *already* are.

He says we are:

- accepted in the Beloved (Ephesians 1:6 NKJV);
- the head, not the tail (Deuteronomy 28:13);

- more than conquerors through Him who loved us (Romans 8:37);
- complete in Him (Colossians 2:10 NKJV);
- free from condemnation (Romans 8:1);
- the righteousness of God (2 Corinthians 5:21);
- and so much more!

I encourage you to start your own search for all the approval and affirmation passages in God's Word before you search someone else on Instagram or Facebook.

The most dangerous aspect of focusing more on your social media profile than on your biblical profile is that what other people approve and affirm in us tends to become what we cling to as self-worth. Over time, these benchmarks of approval and affirmation often override and silence the truth about our worth in Christ and we remain laden with shame or feelings of unworthiness. We attach our self-esteem, purpose, and identity to whatever parts of us get the most endorsements and then we run and hide from any persona that contradicts the part of us who the world applauds. But who God called us to be in our truest form may not be who others approve and affirm. We could be pleasing people all day and not pleasing Him, much like King Saul, who got called out by the prophet Samuel for his approval addiction (1 Samuel 15:24–26). We could be obsessing over admiration from other people and not sense that God is brokenhearted over the choices we're making.

He may be calling you to speak out when others are trying to silence you. He may be nudging you to accept a truth about yourself that is contrary to the words others are feeding you. He may be telling you to stop doing all the things that others expect you to do. We must be willing to find peace in the silence of the crowd so we don't miss the thundering adoration of Him who created and knows the real us.

I wish I could tell you that salvation in Christ fixed my approval addiction instantaneously. Maybe it was like that for some people, but it wasn't the case for me. I would start my day reading and meditating on the approval of His Word, and then I would try to walk it out throughout the day without looking to other people for affirmation, but I couldn't get far. The paralyzing fear that I wasn't good enough kept me on a roller coaster of people-pleasing that made me sick from all the highs and lows of my addiction. If someone besides God told me I was good, I believed I had heard God right and that I *was* good. If someone didn't tell me I was good, I believed I had heard God wrong and that I was anything *but* good.

I was like the Jewish leaders we read about at the end of John 12:

Even after Jesus had performed so many signs in their presence, they still would not believe in Him . . . Yet at the same time many even among the leaders believed in him. But because of the Pharisees they would not openly acknowledge their faith for fear they would be put out of the synagogue; for they loved human praise more than praise from God. (vv. 37, 42–43)

When I first read this passage, I could hear God walking around in the cool of day, coming to teach me a Garden Lesson on approval and affirmation. He knew I was more committed to the sound of human praise than to His voice. He saw the parts of me I was hiding because I was afraid of what others thought of me. The enemy was banking on me staying dependent on adoration and applause outside of God because he knew they were unstable. We humans tend to be fickle and wishy-washy, which makes dependence on human approval an unsafe place to be. People today are still like the folks in Jesus' day who shouted, "Hosanna!" and praised Him on Palm Sunday, then yelled, "Crucify Him!" just days later.

The Garden Lesson God taught me through my approval addiction in the church was that while an endorsement stamp from others is not bad or shameful, it can't ever be our source, the foundation of our lives, or the lens to our faith. Genuine faith is trusting and being satisfied with everything God has for us *in Jesus*, not in others. When we seek the admiration of others as our foundational source, we are seeking our own glory. Jesus said it like this: "How can you believe, when you receive glory from one another and do not seek the glory that comes from the only God?" (John 5:44 ESV).

I love that the Bible makes differential statements like this one that boldly rips through our legalistic thinking. Living a life dependent on other people's approval to silence our own shame is downright miserable. We hand over the control of our joy and our worth to people who are fundamentally unstable in their own joy and worth. The only one who is stable enough to combat our shame is God.

Bound to the Applause

I remember learning a colloquial term that always struck me as the perfect definition of my applause-addicted life. The term "dog and pony show" refers to an overly sensationalized, overdramatic performance or demonstration that goes to great lengths to persuade its audience of its message. Think of an infomercial on steroids and you're close to getting the imagery. The first time I heard that term, I knew it was about me. I was definitely overly sensationalized and overdramatic in trying to convince the world that I was perfect. When God asked me to say goodbye to the dog and pony shows of my life, I didn't realize He also wanted me to say goodbye to a life of slavery to shame and unworthiness that I didn't even realize I was in bondage to.

You know you're a slave to the applause and approval

when you acknowledge that deep inside, some or all your actions and decisions are filtered through who is watching and who isn't. Think about it. Can you operate fully in your life and in your calling if no one is watching? Can you give 100 percent without one hundred likes or views in real life or online? Can you do *you* if no one applauds you?

Can you do *you* if no one applauds you?

Again, I'm not talking about wanting or appreciating recognition from others. I'm talking about needing it so bad that you can't do *you* without someone watching, applauding, or championing you. If you can't honestly admit that you can live your life wholly and completely without the approval and affirmation of even one person, you may be in bondage to approval. If you can't honestly look at stepping back in the doing to enter a season of rest without the fear of what others might think, you may be in bondage to the applause. If you can't hear God's whisper of adoration and validation above the crowds around you and within you, you may be enslaved by affirmation.

I'll never forget what a friend once told me: *If you live for their applause, you will die by their silence.*

Oh, we love great mic-drop lines like that one, huh? I know I do. But who are the "theys" in this statement? Are "they" the parents for whom you never felt good enough? Are "they" the friends who never made you feel accepted or wanted? Are "they" the long list of boyfriends, girlfriends, or ex-husbands who made you believe it was your fault they cheated or walked out? Are "they" the colleagues with whom you compete for positions that you don't even want? Who are "they" in your life?

Whoever "they" are, it's time to let them go. If it's "they" you seek more than God, it's time to serve them notice. Even if "they" are your parents, mentors, pastors, or spouses, you're going to need to let them fall silent and turn your ear again to God and God alone.

Before you think I'm being too harsh or zealous with your "theys," consider that my reference comes directly from Jesus' words in Scripture: "You cannot be my disciple, unless you love me more than you love your father and mother, your wife and children, and your brothers and sisters. You cannot follow me unless you love me more than you love your own life" (Luke 14:26 CEV).

I have had to break up with some "theys" in my life who have been my applaud dealers and praise pushers. To achieve the freedom I needed, I've had to evict some people from my life whose approval and affirmation I thought I couldn't live without. It wasn't easy, and I can't even say people understood why I was saying goodbye to relationships that appeared to feed me, but I knew why. I knew those relationships weren't just feeding me; they were making me a glutton for praise. I couldn't lie to myself anymore. I was addicted, and I needed to get free. It was a liberating but scary season when I walked away from these relationships because I wasn't sure who I was without them. But I knew God couldn't trust me with the more He had for me unless I walked in His freedom and let go of all the people to whom I was in bondage, like my pastors, my leaders, and my followers.

We all need to get free from some "theys" who have taken up too much room in our heads and hearts.

Who are the people in your life who have held you captive to their praise or lack thereof? Who is feeding you or starving you with their approval or disapproval? Whose approval are you still seeking that's keeping you hidden in your own garden? Who are *they*?

Maybe you don't need approval from others. Maybe you need it from *you*.

Sometimes our praise addiction shows up in the way we pursue, obsess, and depend on our own applause. Sometimes, when the people of God get wise to the tricks of the enemy to become applause addicted, he tries the same trap with new bait.

Enter the rise of self-worship in American culture.

Everyone, including professionals and experts, would agree that self-acceptance and self-affirmation is beneficial to our mental health, and while the sentiment is great, we need to be careful not to lose ourselves in the trap of self-worship. The enemy is always trying to get us to focus on ourselves to the same degree some people focus on pleasing others. The result is still shame. But as believers, we can be God-focused, which brings freedom. The temptation to self-worship is to feed our souls by ourselves from within ourselves. But our souls are only truly fed by God.

As the global and local church, we aren't called to approve and affirm ourselves. We are called to bring praise to Jesus, our Savior who loved us and gave Himself as a ransom for us.

Remember, *praise* and *validation* are not cusswords. We've been called to be voices of encouragement to others by recognizing and honoring one another to bring glory to the work that God is doing in their lives. Our children and grandchildren need to see, hear, and feel what authentic and healthy applause sounds like so they can break the cycle of addiction to likes, follows, clicks, and views. Our families and communities need to hear approval and affirmation that utilizes language that applauds the God at work in them. Our churches need people who are willing to help others take off their graveclothes of judgment and disapproval so they can see Jesus and hear His approval and affirmation.

Friend, I want to be a voice of freedom to you now. No one's approval or affirmation will ever compare to the approval and affirmation of your God. Nothing will ever feed your soul to overflow like the love and adoration of our Father who sees past your shame to the real you He created from the beginning. You can come out of your cave because everything you need, everything you seek, and everything you crave is in Him and in the plans and purposes He penned in love before you ever breathed your first breath. He is pleased with you as His son or daughter.

You could do nothing further in your life from this moment on and God's seal of approval on you still wouldn't change. You could make mistake after mistake and the shame you battle wouldn't have any effect on the way He sees you, loves you, and wants you. He isn't like the voices and opinions you once sought. He is the One who saw you then and sees you now.

Let His approval wash over the countless disapprovals you've lived with for far too long.

Let His affirmation flood your heart and mind to enable you to believe His truth more than the lies you've believed for too many days, months, and years.

Let His praise over you draw you out of your cave of hiding so He can free you from the bondage of the applause-masters in your life.

Let His rejoicing over you settle you and reassure you of His delight in you (Zephaniah 3:17).

And above all, let yourself receive the freedom He paid for you to have.

You're not a slave to approval.

You're not what shame has affirmed about you.

You're not worthless without someone's praise.

You're God's, and that is more than enough. You're the one He wanted and still wants to this day. You're the one

He looked for in the garden and the one He still looks for. You're the one He called good and the one He still sees as good in Christ Jesus. You're the one and you've always been the one—with or without the applause of man, the affirmation of society, or the praise of the world.

And all that you are in Him has always been enough and will always be enough for Him.

So let today be the day you start living free in Him and for Him.

Be free, my friend. Be free.

Garden Meditation

Give yourself some quiet moments before the Lord to seek out honest answers to these questions. Don't answer them the way you think they should be answered, but let go of approval and welcome honesty, transparency, and vulnerability.

- Where are you addicted to approval and affirmation? How does it show up in your everyday life? What are your affirmation triggers?
- How does your value for what you do relate to your value for who you *are* when you are in high-achievement mode? What about when you do absolutely nothing?
- How do you respond to the presence or absence of applause, admiration, power, or status?

SPEAKING FIRE INTO YOUR APPROVAL IN CHRIST

I declare I will choose God's approval over man's approval as I meditate on God's affirmations over my life [1 Thessalonians 2:4]. I will use my energy not to fear or worry about other people but to believe by faith in the God who believes in me [Psalm 118:6–9]. I seek Him and Him alone, knowing that everything else I need will be added to my life [Matthew 6:33].

Boundaries

The Power of No

Every June when I was growing up, my sisters and I would pack our bags and kiss our daddy goodbye to go stay with our mom for the three months of summer vacation. Growing up in a two-household family meant our lives were not only split geographically but also influentially. We lived under two different parenting styles, experiences, and decision-making philosophies. Both sets had their own benefits and dysfunctions, and both were extremes.

At our dad's we were parented in structure and had a very sheltered day-to-day experience. We didn't even own a television set until our late teens because my dad valued the nurturing of our minds. He believed watching television hindered our ability to think for ourselves, so the TVs stayed out and the rules stayed in.

With Mom we had access in excess to any and every pleasure we desired and were essentially able to do whatever we wanted as long as we weren't harming ourselves or others. Mom's work schedule took over her days, so we were often left to our own devices from dawn to dusk without any parental oversight. All we did was find ways to occupy our time until she got back home.

Early on, we got acquainted with our neighbors. They had a daughter around the same age as our nephew, whom my mom took in to raise when the responsibility of parenthood became too much for my older brother to bear. Mom's neighbors had a trampoline and a backyard pool, which beat the television we watched for hours as if we were catching up on the nine months we were without a TV at my dad's house.

Our neighbors became like family; we were often told we didn't have to knock before going inside and were welcome in their home whenever we wanted. The dad always paid special attention to us girls and invoked weird feelings I had never felt before. He told me often that I was pretty and funny. He laughed at my jokes, asked me how my day was, and always made me feel seen.

I had no boundaries or supervision. What I did have was a narrative in my young mind that repeatedly told me

I was unlovable. It was the perfect storm for a tornado of inappropriate affection, unwanted attention, and unmerited shame. I was an easy target. Our neighbor picked up on it and preyed on me.

By age twelve I had been groomed unknowingly by this man for over three years, and I was at his mercy. That was the year he convinced me that I wanted to give him my innocence. He manipulated me to such a degree that I actually believed it was my choice and desire to give up my virginity to a married man more than twice my age. The shame that ensued from what was done and the mental torment of thinking it was something I welcomed and wanted drove me to a dark place that I vowed I would never let anyone take me to again.

It was a big promise for such a little girl.

My lack of parental boundaries became a lack of physical, mental, and emotional boundaries until I found myself burdened by the weight of shame that was never mine to carry. I was a child, and I had no reason to feel shame for the actions of the adults in my life, but I still carried it well into adulthood. By that point I had learned I could carry it a little easier thanks to the help of drugs and denial. If no one had set boundaries for me as a child to keep me safe, why did I need them as an adult?

Many years later, I went back to visit my mom and found myself at one of her famous house parties. We had a backyard full of people when, suddenly, my abuser's wife started aggressively shaming one of my family members. Profane words and accusations were spewing out of her mouth as she publicly shamed her in front of everyone—calling her a home-wrecker and worse. She waved a love letter that had been hidden among her husband's possessions in which my family member professed her love for him and her eagerness for the day they could be together.

It was a scene to be seen.

Come to find out, the husband had been visiting the young woman at her college campus on weekends and had her convinced she was in love with him. As with me, he had groomed her and robbed her of her innocence, but she was the one being shamed for all the world to see. The craziest part was that this young girl just sat there, condemned and full of shame, taking all the venom coming from this pedophile's wife's mouth, completely unaware that *she* was a victim.

At that moment something came over me and I shouted, "She is not the names you're calling her! *She* is a victim! He did it to me too! He did it to me too! When I was only twelve!" The secret I'd thought I would take to my grave was exposed when the pain of seeing someone else bound was greater than my own shame. Chaos immediately turned to silence as the wife was confronted with the truth that she was married to a child molester and a monster—not a faithful, innocent husband.

When I broke my silence about what had happened, the truth liberated more than just me. It exposed that the man had brought about the same horrific trauma on other young girls, one of whom was his own daughter, who he abused when she was just eight years old. Incredulously, she had the courage to break her own silence when my voice put words to the story she had been too scared to speak. My voice spoke for her when hers had been taken and prompted her to keep speaking after I spoke.

In 2 Corinthians the Bible paints a beautiful picture that when you are in Christ, the old places of shame are gone, and behold, you have been made new! "Therefore, if anyone is in Christ, the new creation has come: The old has gone, the new is here!" (5:17).

Shame will make you hold on to things from the past as though they determine your value in the present, but you're beyond that lie. Shame will make you hide parts of your testimony out of fear that you will be judged, but God wants to use all of your testimony to help set other people free. God will use everything you've been through if you allow Him to.

You may think your identity without shame only brings freedom to you, but that's not true.

Don't you realize that your story is tied to someone else's liberation?

Maybe you're like I was, and you think you're going to take your shame story to the grave. But your story is not just yours to own; it's yours to share. And the freer you get, the more you help others find their voices, their identities, and their freedom too.

And the freer you get, the more you help others find their voices, their identities, and their freedom too.

In some cases boundaries have a negative connotation, but the boundaries God puts in place are intended to protect us and keep us safe—not to limit our freedom. Most people struggle to appreciate the protective hand of God, but those same people struggle without the presence of His hand as well. We want God; we just don't always want to be tied to God.

The truth is, God's original boundaries were always part of our freedom, not our punishment. His vision was always for us to live in the freedom He died for us to have.

The enemy uses our natural curiosity to continually tempt us to cross boundaries that God has given us. Satan tries to make us think that we know better or need to know better, when the biblical principle of John 10:10 is in operation anytime he speaks to us: "The thief comes only to steal and kill and destroy."

His existential job is to steal from us, kill us, and destroy us. There is not one part of him that wants to add to our lives. His objective is purely to take from us what God gave us freely. Without boundaries to safeguard us from his lies and deceit, we end up handing over what we never intended to give up. You may think those boundaries you hate aren't there for your benefit, but they are. I didn't think I wanted boundaries as a young girl, but they would have safeguarded me from succumbing to a lie that walked right into my boundaryless life.

Without boundaries, trust can never fully develop because untested faith is merely hope. We can hope we'll color within the lines, but without the lines we'll never know if we venture beyond the borders. It doesn't sound like anything major when we're talking about crayons and coloring pages, but it's the same principle when the stakes are higher. We all hope we'll do the right thing when we need to, but it isn't until we have the decision in front of us that we will know what choice we'll make.

In my case my parents never would have hoped for their daughter to fall victim to a predator like my neighbor, but when they had the choice, they didn't draw the line. There was no malicious or neglectful intent. They simply missed their chance to draw a line I was too young to draw for myself.

Isn't that exactly how it is for all of us?

We don't mean to venture off too far in one direction, but without a boundary line we can't truly see how far out of the lines we've gone. We don't intend to let something harmless become something harmful, but without a boundary we don't know how far is too far. We would never willingly allow an intruder into our personal space, but we're an open target without a line to differentiate personal space from open space.

When we trust that Jesus truly came to give us life in abundance (John 10:10), we can begin to trust the boundaries God has given us through His written Word and the Holy Spirit's leading. Boundaries aren't just things God has written for us in His Word, but they are also lines He has drawn through the leading of the Spirit. *You don't have to do that, say that, or believe that. You can say no to that, Mariela.*

What's God telling you right now about a certain situation or person?

Is He telling you to get off social media for a season because it's a stumbling block for you?

Is He telling you to unfollow certain profiles on social media because they lead you to comparison?

Is He telling you to leave *that* relationship alone because it leads you right into temptation every time?

These are all boundaries. And the crayon is in your hand.

The choice to draw a line is up to you.

The choice to honor that line is also up to you.

No More Trees of Shame

As our relationship with God grows stronger and our relationship with shame grows weaker, we will more easily and readily honor and obey God's boundaries because we realize He who created them for us is just that: *for us.*

He's not against us or trying to run a game on us. He's not behind a tree in the garden just waiting to jump out and say, "Gotcha!" He's for us in every sense of the word.

If we're truly going to embrace a shame-free life, we need to understand and accept that boundaries are essential.

Adam and Eve had boundaries in the garden, designed for their good, to keep them protected and safe from an eternity of shame, but they made a choice and crossed a boundary and consequently ushered in shame. The entire garden was theirs to name, rule, and possess, but all that freedom came with one very distinct boundary: "And the LORD God commanded the man, 'You are free to eat from any tree in the garden; but you must not eat from the tree of the knowledge of good and evil, for when you eat from it you will certainly die'" (Genesis 2:16–17).

If we're truly going to embrace a shame-free life, we need to understand and accept that boundaries are essential.

This boundary was the one boundary that mattered. Maybe you feel that you have all the boundaries you need, and you follow them to a *t*. If so, save this chapter for that one time a boundary line gets a little blurry for you.

Keep in mind, God's boundaries aren't blurry in any way. We might blur them, but He doesn't.

In God's original plan, He told Adam clearly, "Hey, see this line? Don't cross it. You won't like what's on the other side, so I'm trying to save you from all that." God didn't make it confusing or convoluted. He told Adam exactly where the boundary line was and made sure that Adam had everything he needed within his boundary. Crystal clear. So it's interesting to me that it wasn't Adam who took the first step (or bite) across the boundary; it was Eve.

Since Eve wasn't yet created when God clearly outlined His garden boundaries to Adam, that tells me one of three things:

1. Adam wasn't a good communicator of boundaries.

Or

2. Eve wasn't a good listener when it came to boundaries.

Or

3. Eve was a good listener, but in the moment of temptation, she didn't care that she was crossing a boundary.

When dealing with boundaries, we are either the communicator or the listener, and our ability to be both is critical to living shame-free lives.

If we can't communicate what we need to the people we love most, how do we provide safeguards for them to follow? They need to hear exactly what we need them to do or not do and what will happen if they choose not to respect our line. Being clear in communication when it comes to boundaries gives others a road map they can follow to avoid the pitfalls others may see but they don't. Let's look at a couple of possible scenarios.

In scenario 1, Adam would have failed to give Eve a heads-up about the God he knew behind the boundary. Since she wasn't created when God communicated to Adam, we're assuming she was fully dependent on Adam to communicate God's boundaries. If he didn't, it means he kept her in the dark instead of bringing her into the know of relationship with God.

She got the information, but not the spirit behind the information.

If it was Adam's poor communication that led to the fall, I've got to believe that if Eve had known the spirit behind the information, she would have been more likely to throw that fruit right back at that lying serpent. But in scenario 2, maybe Adam did communicate it with all the urgency and intention that it was spoken to him. Maybe Eve just didn't listen with that same urgency and intention.

If we don't heed the warnings from those who give us boundaries, what right do we have to get mad or frustrated at unnecessary struggles we ourselves have created? With those we trust, we need to have open ears, open minds, and open hearts to boundaries that are drawn for us so that we can glean from the wisdom and direction of others. When we can listen and accept a no from someone else, it saves us from saying yes to something we should be saying no to.

Our ability to communicate and listen to boundaries either sets us free from shame or perpetuates our shame.

When we are born again into the body of Christ, we face garden moments every day. We are given the choice whether to eat of the Tree of Knowledge of Good and Evil with every decision. We are given the choice to listen or to ignore. We are given the choice to do what we think is right or to obey what God has already said. The Bible says, "There is a way that seems right to a man, but its end is the way of death" (Proverbs 14:12 NKJV).

Let's just stop for a confessional moment before we get caught in thinking we are holier than we actually are when it comes to boundaries.

None of us like to be told no. We all like the freedom to do what we want, when we want, and how we want. Many of us are content with making Jesus our Savior, but we haven't granted Him full access to be our Lord.

What's the difference? Here's one way to understand lordship: If you rent, who do you pay? A landlord, right? The landlord calls the shots since you are living in his or her property. Well, you have been bought by the blood of Jesus, and His lordship means you understand that you are no longer your own—He calls the shots. The beautiful thing about Him calling the shots is that His shots are always just, kind, compassionate, loyal, faithful, and true. He is the best landlord ever. He won't evict you. He won't make you pay a cost He's already paid. He won't change the contract.

Our willingness and desire to obey the boundaries God gives us show whether Jesus is only our Savior or also our Lord.

God's lordship over your life doesn't just give you freedom. It also passes on the grace to live out that freedom every day in every decision.

The life of freedom God has for us to enjoy on this side of heaven is one that is protected by His Word. Through grace, we can live a shame-free life within the confines and safety of the finished work of Christ. Which really means, His grace empowers us to obey and live free from condemnation whenever we miss the mark. But that's not just my opinion or experience. It's biblical:

> For the grace of God has appeared that offers salvation to all people. It teaches us to say "No" to ungodliness and worldly passions, and to live self-controlled, upright and godly lives in this present age, while we wait for the blessed hope—the appearing of the glory of our great God and Savior, Jesus Christ, who gave himself for us to redeem us from all wickedness and to purify for himself a people that are his very own, eager to do what is good. (Titus 2:11–14)

As we dive deeper into who He is and how His boundaries liberate us, we begin to truly understand what God meant when He said through the prophet, "'For my thoughts are not your thoughts, neither are your ways my ways,' declares the LORD. 'As the heavens are higher than the earth, so are my ways higher than your ways and my thoughts than your thoughts'" (Isaiah 55:8–9).

When we realize we don't have to understand His boundaries to obey them, it makes it easier for us to see things from His perspective instead of ours. The battle to do what we want ceases because we understand and accept His ways without a mentality that wars against Him. The struggle to obey or not to obey ends because we realize we want to live from God's perspective instead of trying to make Him come down to our perspectives. We move and operate in the ways of the kingdom because we trust the King. We adhere to the boundaries of God because we operate from the law of love that gives us the grace to obey, rather than the law of legalism that withholds the grace to obey.

It was the law of love—not the law of legalism—that covered Adam and Eve in the garden.

It was the law of love—not the law of legalism—that carried Jesus from heaven to the cross and back to heaven for us.

It was the law of love—not the law of legalism—that teaches us how to live in the grace we find in the New Testament.

The Higher Perspective

In Proverbs 25:28 the author used the analogy of a city and its walls to offer insight on personal boundary-making,

"Like a city whose walls are broken through is a person who lacks self-control."

This verse clearly communicates to us that biblical boundaries are tied to self-control. We don't have to live long to know that adhering to boundaries requires a certain amount of self-control, but that doesn't mean we understand the full implications of ignoring them. We all could benefit from graduating to the thinking that the first person who needs to hear our no is us when our flesh wants to say yes. Creating healthy personal boundaries allows us to honor ourselves and others well by being real with what's healthy and unhealthy for us. Our one no just might help us avoid or escape the shame of a thousand yeses we never meant to say.

Have you ever heard the phrase, "If you don't stand for something, you will fall for anything"? Well, if you don't know where you end and others begin, then by default, you will always compromise on who you really are and what you believe. A clear boundary with yourself is essentially taking the higher ground and saying, "This is my territory, and you can't just come up in here like that."

Our culture loves a good boundary—even if it's only one-sided. We love being able to hold our line and demand people respect our no without the need to reciprocate the same for others. As a matter of fact, there is such a rise in this boundary discussion that some healthy boundaries have become unhealthy boundaries in disguise. Drawing a relational line out of unresolved conflict, anger, or punishment becomes a way for toxicity to spread like a cancer in the name of healthy boundaries, and it has seeped into our homes, our workplaces, our schools, and the church. How many of these places have suffered because we've placed a permanent boundary instead of utilizing conflict management and communication?

Boundary conversations have become a cloak of fig leaves for an offended heart that refuses to forgive and heal. The law says an eye for an eye (Leviticus 24:19–21), but the law of love says forgive seventy times seven (Matthew 18:21–22).

Grace calls us to have a higher perspective, not to remain offended and cut someone out of our life and call it a boundary. We, as believers, cannot take on the same narrative of cutting people out of our lives as the world does, slap Jesus' name on it, and expect the blessings to rain down.

Only you can search your heart and ask yourself in total honesty if you have created boundaries with people because you simply have unresolved issues and just don't want to deal with them. Only you can bring health to toxic boundaries.

"Mariela, are you saying I need to just let anyone back into my life after an offense because I am a Christian?"

No. *Heck no.* I am saying to make sure you've forgiven that person and released him or her with a boundary instead of punishing the offender and banishing him or her with your unforgiveness.

Okay, so the next question you probably have is, How do you know if you have forgiven someone? Here's what

I've learned from all my hidden, shameful places that didn't come with boundaries. You know you have forgiven someone when that individual can be in your presence and you don't feel that he or she owes you anything and you feel free. That person can walk in without either of you feeling controlled by fear and walk out without leaving you paralyzed by fear. It's from that place that you can create the boundary accordingly, if one needs to be made.

The boundaries of the garden show us that we were not created to live outside of healthy boundaries, but that those boundaries were drawn with the pen of protection, not the pen of punishment.

If you feel as though you can't rebuild the boundaries in your life, remember this: Jesus had boundaries too. He ministered to the multitudes but shared intimacy with only a select few. He modeled this need to have boundaries by the circle of people He kept close and the circles of people He kept at a distance. He showed us by example that there is power and purpose in having circles for the many and circles for the few.

Healthy boundaries are established when we know who we are and live our lives with intention and purpose. Jesus knew who He was and why He was here. Scripture tells us on multiple occasions that He would draw away from people to be alone with His Father.

Did His drawing a line with people make Him mean and unloving? No. However, this thought seems to be a prevailing false narrative believed by many Christians who are trying to figure out how to establish healthy boundaries. Somewhere along the way, we started buying into the lie that we should always be available because that's the loving thing to do. That narrative paints an unrealistic expectation none of us can uphold, so shame becomes the by-product.

If you have been caught in that trap, I pray you receive freedom right now in Jesus' name. Healthy boundaries are reestablished when you understand and accept that sometimes other people need your no more than your yes.

There will always be times when you and I will need to say no. Use those times to learn how valuable your no is so you can color your life inside the lines as the Holy Spirit speaks to you. And as He gives you the grace and courage to live from an honest yes or no, begin to experience the fire you speak.

Your yes has fire.

Your no has fire.

Your life has fire when you can use both.

Let's face it: we can't go back and change what happened to Adam and Eve by trying to overcompensate for their disregard of boundaries. But while we can't go back to safeguard their boundaries, we can change what happens in our garden now. If you're not sure how to create healthy boundaries, let me share with you some of the lines I've drawn that have safeguarded my relationship with God, others, and myself.

Create boundaries around the thoughts you allow
yourself to meditate on (2 Corinthians 10:5).

Create boundaries on what you allow yourself to
take in mentally and emotionally (Proverbs 4:23;
Romans 12:2).

Create boundaries around what comes out of your
mouth (Psalm 141:3).

Create boundaries around what comes into your ears
(Proverbs 2:2).

Create boundaries that draw you closer to God (James
4:8).

Create boundaries around devotional habits and
routines (Joshua 1:8).

Create boundaries around the convictions you stand
for and defend (Joshua 24:15).

Create boundaries around your identity and purpose
(Matthew 5:14–16).

Create boundaries based on God's revealed Word
(Psalm 119:11; Luke 11:28).

Create boundaries that will

_____ (_____).

Create boundaries that give you

_____ (_____).

Create boundaries that challenge you to

_____ (_____).

These boundaries will help you reclaim the areas that

got handed over to shame with or without your consent. You don't have to stay trapped in hidden places without a voice anymore. You're not who you were when you first encountered shame, so let's start drawing some lines that represent the free you, the no-longer-shamed you. There is a greater work of grace in you that is teaching you lessons on how to say yes to living from your healthy, shame-free self.

Say yes to God's leading and His loving.

Say yes to His forgiving and His welcoming.

Say yes to His boundaries and His undoing of boundaries not of His making.

Say yes to His boundaries and experience freedom from the ravages of shame.

Say yes because you can, not because you must.

Garden Reflection

Put a boundary on this time and space and give yourself the freedom to go deeper into this conversation with God.

- Do you have secrets that have shackled you to shame? If you vowed to take them to the grave, as I did, what would it look like to break one of these vows and break into freedom? Who would be liberated by your story?
- How did you feel when I gave you a list of boundaries to create in your life? Are you afraid to say no

and draw those lines? Do you feel empowered to find your voice again and take back the pen of your life to rewrite your boundaries? How can you dive deeper into the source and motivation behind these powerful emotions?

- Where is your boundary line with God? Have you drawn a line around Him that keeps Him near or far? Is that where you need Him or want Him?

SPEAKING FIRE INTO YOUR BOUNDARIES

I declare the Spirit of God dwells within me and gives me the courage to let my yes be yes and my no be no [Matthew 5:37; 1 Corinthians 3:16]. Today, and in the days ahead, I will examine my choices so that I will not repeat the errors of the past but instead live in a future that is based on pleasing God and trusting His timing [Proverbs 3:5–6].

GARDEN
LESSON
Six

Senses

The Battle Between Flesh and Spirit

I started my ministry in 2018 with the simple mission to encourage people in the Lord. I loved having an outlet to share what the Lord was teaching me and was blessed to know I could potentially partner with Him to help others on their journey. I can say that everything that came from my ministry was birthed from a pure place that found its origins in obedience to God. He called me to start She Speaks Fire, so I did. There was a grace over my life to post daily on social media from an overflow of my heart, and I carried a sense of purpose and joy in the process.

It wasn't burdensome; it wasn't heavy; it was good.

Call me naive if you want, but I legit had no idea there was a whole world in the online space of writers who created profiles with the intention of being discovered or platforms that would gain them influence and eventually become a business and source of income. Now, don't mishear what I am saying. There is nothing wrong with starting a business and making money—but I seriously had no clue! Suddenly, I found myself in a community of writers, poets, and creatives I never knew existed. I didn't see myself in them, but there was something familiar about them that resonated with me.

I was happily in my lane, delighting in the Lord and encouraging His people, when my eyes were opened and I saw what I hadn't seen initially. I saw other women like me with platforms that were doing big things. I saw that they each had an email newsletter, free downloads, conferences, courses, memberships, and more. Something in me started to want what I was seeing. And just like that, I went from being led by the Spirit to being led by my flesh—or my senses. Like Eve did in the garden: "The woman was convinced. She saw that the tree was beautiful and its fruit looked delicious, and she wanted the wisdom it would give her. So she took some of the fruit and ate it. Then she gave some to her husband, who was with her, and he ate it, too" (Genesis 3:6 NLT).

Like Eve, I saw something and perceived that it was good. I saw women killing it on social media, and it didn't just look good, it looked beautiful. I wanted the impact I believed they were having. So I took in some of their fruit and ate it. Not a big bite. Just a harmless little nibble. I began striving and building something that God hadn't instructed me to build and working myself to the bone only to be left with heaping loads of shame because deep down I knew I'd started working apart from God.

I was ashamed that I could not stay consistent writing the email newsletter God hadn't told me to write.

I was ashamed that I couldn't keep up with a social media posting schedule God hadn't told me to create.

I was ashamed that I hadn't developed a course or established a membership that God hadn't told me to take on.

Shame, shame, and more shame.

Shame told me I was a failure and a joke to my community, so I retreated. I stopped posting and hid for close to a year, paralyzed because I had followed my senses instead of God's Spirit. I understood all too well the "nothing" Jesus was talking about when He said, "I am the vine; you are the branches. If you remain in me and I in you, you will bear much fruit; apart from me you can do nothing" (John 15:5).

What things in your life are you doing without God's guidance?

What ways have seemed right to you, but led you to a place that you had no business being?

Eve went from hanging out in Paradise with her man, having freedom of purpose and fellowship with God, to coveting something she perceived was good but that led her outside of God's will.

Does this sound familiar?

Have you ever taken your focus off what God gave you to pursue something you perceived was better than what you already had?

Have you ever gone your own way only to discover a spiritual and emotional death that led to

death in your purpose?

death in your relationship with others?

death in your relationship with God?

If so, you are not alone. Welcome to the club. We live in a digital age in which we are inundated with sensory overload and the constant temptation to covet, compete, and compare. Our eyes become gateways to shame because we're flooded with images, ideas, and illusions of grandeur aimed at creating an appetite for things we don't currently have. Even more problematic, these images blind us to what we *do* have. Allowing our eyes to lead us becomes a prescription for some unhealthy shame—shame for what we want and shame for not seeing the blessings in what we have.

In Christ we have all we need pertaining to life and godliness (2 Peter 1:3). Did you hear that? We have *all* things—just as Eve did in the garden. She had knowledge and wisdom because she had God, who in Himself is

Wisdom. But the enemy tricked her into believing she needed what she already had. The answer will always be to focus on what we have and not the things around us that we think we need. When we allow ourselves to be led by our physical senses, we rob ourselves of what God has for us in the Spirit.

In Christ we have all we need pertaining to life and godliness.

Our natural senses can fool us and make us unknowingly fallible. I doubt Eve knew that following her natural senses would lead to the fall of humanity and the introduction of shame to all the world, but here we are. As believers we know there is more to this life and this world than what we see around us. As the writer of Hebrews put it, "By faith we understand that the universe was formed at God's command, so that what is seen was not made out of what was visible" (11:3).

Yet repeatedly we are led by what we see, hear, taste, touch, and smell. We focus on what our senses are reporting to us about our identities, purpose, and faith without considering that so much more is happening in the unseen realm.

Without a sold-out belief that we are toggling between the seen and the unseen, nothing that I am about to share will make any sense to you. I'm about to sound real crazy to some folks who don't quite know where they stand when it comes to spiritual warfare. But I ask that you give me a shot as we explore some thoughts you may not have considered before.

First, let me say that I believe the enemy of our souls wants those who openly talk about spiritual warfare to be dubbed "hyperspiritual" as a way to discredit them.

But there is certainly a spiritual aspect to the world in which we live. God told Adam, "You must not eat from the tree of the knowledge of good and evil, for when you eat from it you will certainly die" (Genesis 2:17). Did Adam and Eve drop dead the moment they ate from the tree? No, they did not. God wasn't talking about an immediate physical death that is perceived with our natural senses. While their sin did lead to their physical deaths later, He was talking about a spiritual death that can only be perceived through that which is unseen. Shame was ushered into the story of humanity through the enticement of Adam and Eve's natural senses. If we are going to battle shame, we need to understand what is really going on, because everything is not always as it seems.

A Spiritual Battle

Transitions have never been great moments for me. I'm not a fan of changes that put me in situations where I feel uncertain and unnerved. Some people thrive on the unexpected and the unknown. I'm not one of those people. So when it came time for me to start high school, I was not as excited as I made people believe. I was terrified. What if I didn't make any new friends? What if my old friends didn't want to hang out with me anymore? What if I wasn't smart enough for my classes? What if the teachers hated me and my people-pleasing self? What if every single day was a repeat of my tenth birthday party?

The closer I got to my first day of high school, the more my inner dread increased. I played out every scenario I could think of to mentally prepare myself. It was the worst summer for me because every day was filled with worry, anxiety, and terror. No one knew my torment because I put on a smile when anyone asked if I was excited to go to high school. In my mind I already hated everything about high school, and I hadn't even walked through the front door yet. The first day came and school started. But it was nothing like I thought it would be. I made friends. I loved my teachers. I played sports and joined the cheer team. I loved every second of my high school years.

I have thought often about the terror that consumed my mind that summer. Why was I so afraid? Now that I am more aware of the unseen tactics of the enemy and how he works to control us, I know that the warfare I battled in my mind was real. The enemy whispered lies to keep me bound in fear. I can still hear his taunting that I wouldn't be popular or do well academically. It sounds silly that satan would spend time tormenting a teenage girl about a high school experience, but it wasn't. It was strategic, and by the grace of God, it didn't work.

Imagine if all my worst nightmares had come true or that I had gone to school so deeply paralyzed in fear that I sabotaged my own experience. Maybe I wouldn't have gone to college. Maybe I wouldn't have had people speak life into me and into my future. Maybe I would have given up and who I am today would be an entirely different Mariela. Maybe I wouldn't have survived.

And all those maybes would have added up to me living in bondage to shame had I let my senses get the best of me.

This is why I fight so hard to speak hope to young people today who are battling shame, suicidal thoughts, depression, and anxiety. I speak against the false accusations and lies the enemy may be sending to them. I know their torment and I know it isn't always fabricated in a young person's mind. The enemy assaults us with negative thoughts, and it's the unseen places in our minds that can cause a shift of destiny, a shift of identity, or a shift of purpose in our lives.

As believers we need to be aware that we live in two very real and highly active worlds: the earthly realm and the heavenly realm. It is to this end that Paul reminded us, "Our struggle is not against flesh and blood, but against the rulers, against the authorities, against the powers of this dark world and against the spiritual forces of evil in the heavenly realms" (Ephesians 6:12).

In other words, the things that are taking place in our

visible and physical world connect to what is happening in the spiritual world. The war that is being waged in the heavenly realms and the direct implications it has on our lives as believers gives us insight into what is really happening behind the scenes of our relationships, our churches, and the problems we face. Through Scripture, God gives us a sneak peek behind the scenes to reveal who is pulling the shame strings. Our human perception can only take us so far, which is why we need to tap in spiritually to be able to see more of the picture.

This might sound very overwhelming and discouraging. But please remember that ultimately, the battle is not ours but the Lord's (2 Chronicles 20:15). The sooner we understand that we are truly in the throes of a spiritual war that was being waged long before we ever stepped foot on planet Earth, the sooner we will be able to navigate life with eyes wide open and an unshakable confidence in who we are because we know whose we are. And, yes, we are in a war, but we are in a war that has already been won! Yes, we fight against the weapons of our enemy, but we fight *from* victory, not *for* it.

The reason we get tripped up and enticed by our physical senses the way Eve did in the garden is because there is a well-crafted plan to shift our focus from what is real and eternal toward what is physical and temporary. This life is but "a vapor that appears for a little while, and then vanishes away" (James 4:14 NASB). Not only is our time on earth temporary; earth is not our home! We are "foreigners and exiles" who are called to "abstain from sinful desires, which wage war against your soul" (1 Peter 2:11). For Christians, the world's ways are not our ways because our citizenship is in heaven, not earth. In the same way we might be tempted by new sights and smells while visiting a foreign country, our spiritual senses here in our natural state are constantly being tempted by carnal things that aren't part of heaven.

Our senses drive us toward the destination of our own desires into shame, or away from them and into freedom. What do I mean by that?

Well, first, Eve saw the tree, but then she desired what the tree could give her. Scripture says that before eating of its fruit, "she wanted the wisdom it would give her" (Genesis 3:6 NLT). Another translation says she saw it was "desirable to make one wise" (NASB).

Desire is a powerful thing, and when it's misplaced in the things of this world, it brings forth shame and destruction. I am not trying to be dramatic. I am warning you because it's the truth. Eve was drawn away by what she saw and tempted to sin through her desire for something outside of God's will for her. Sin and shame happened in the blink of an eye. The same goes for us if we allow our senses and desires to drive our lives. The Bible gives us this warning about desires: "Temptation comes from our own desires, which entice us and drag us away. These desires give birth to sinful actions. And when sin is allowed to grow, it gives birth to death" (James 1:14–15 NLT).

What is it that you desire? And further, have these desires of the flesh led you to experience shame?

In the world in which we live, we tend to be motivated and governed by our worldly desires—desires that don't come from the Father. In 1 John this is called loving the world and what it offers: "For everything in the world—the lust of the flesh, the lust of the eyes, and the pride of life—comes not from the Father but from the world" (2:16).

Believers' desires were never intended to be shaped by what our culture deems valuable and desirable. They were always intended to be shaped by Jesus and what He revealed to this world as valuable to our Father in heaven. But when our desires get the best of us and we fall prey to pursuing things apart from God, it's harder to return to the hands of the Potter, and we start to shape ourselves, unwittingly molding shame into the clay of our lives.

So my next question to you is, What do you love more than God?

We are less likely to be drawn away by what we see when our love and affection are set on Him who we cannot see. No matter where your desires have led you, it's not too late to make a U-turn back to the Father.

If you find yourself desiring your own way and chasing physical pleasure . . . repent and turn the other way.

If you find yourself desiring the things you see and wanting everything for yourself . . . repent and turn the other way.

If you find yourself desiring to appear important while taking pride in your own achievements and possessions . . . repent and turn the other way.

Now, I know all that sounds like an old-school approach to the desires that lead us to shame's front door, but there is real value in old-school wisdom. Genesis 1 tells us that Adam and Eve were made in the very image of God—without flaws, without defects, and without any knowledge or experience of guilt or shame. All they desired was the goodness, the provision, the promises, and the protection of God. They had no conscious awareness to desire anything different. They woke up every day fulfilled with purpose, empowered with authority, and confident in their relationship with their Father. They had no space in their senses for an awareness of anything other than the knowledge that they were complete and whole in Him. It wasn't until the serpent told them something was missing that they went against God's will and experienced shame.

How much of your relationship with shame is the result of someone telling you something is missing? What wouldn't you tolerate in your mind and emotions if you knew without a doubt that you were not a slave to your desires and senses?

Answering those questions honestly takes the scales off our eyes and pulls back the curtain of shame.

Pulling Back the Curtain of Shame

When I first came to faith, I was in a relationship that did not glorify God. Before even knowing the word *fornicate* or what it meant, I felt a gentle nudge in my spirit to quit having sex with my boyfriend. I didn't know what the nudge was or where it was coming from, but I knew that what I was doing didn't feel right, and I didn't want to do it anymore.

When I shared this with my boyfriend, he was less than excited. He tried to convince me that having sex wasn't that big of a deal since we had already done it. He told me that since we loved each other, sex was a natural expression of our love. To him, marriage was just a piece of paper, and his rationale was that we were committed to each other. *I do love him*, I thought, and what he said really did make sense. We *were* committed to each other. And what would really change from today to tomorrow if we got married? *It is just a piece of paper.* So I ignored the prompting I felt inside and followed the desires of my flesh. I know now that the Holy Spirit was nudging me, but back then, my desire to be wanted, loved, and accepted led me away from God and drew me deeper into my battle with shame.

If you're like me and lean toward seeking external validation and love, the enemy will send someone who will affirm you while drawing you away from God. I think many of us are expecting the enemy of our souls to jump out with a pitchfork and red horns, but what if I told you he doesn't work like that? Oftentimes we experience his influence in the things we desire most. Spiritual warfare does not show favoritism or partiality, and we are all open to attack at some point, like it or not. Your life is a gift from God, but you are also a walking target for the enemy, the one who seeks to steal, kill, and destroy (John 10:10). But there is good news! The Bible reminds us that greater is He who is in us than he who is in the world (1 John 4:4).

Jesus has overcome the darkness of shame, and you can stand on the words the prophet Isaiah spoke: "No weapon formed against you shall prosper" (Isaiah 54:17 NKJV).

Notice, the weapons won't prosper—but that doesn't mean they won't form!

Shame is a weapon, which means we must fight against it. God has given us the tools and guidance on how to do this through His living Word. He has given us our opponent's playbook. We have a cheat sheet! Satan has no new tricks since his first appearance in the Bible. As a matter of fact, he is a one-trick pony. The only power that he has is the power we give him through our own inability, indifference, or straight-up refusal to open our spiritual eyes.

Notice, the weapons won't prosper—but that doesn't mean they won't form!

The evil one has a strategy. He will convince you to do something contrary to God's will and then accuse you afterward so you experience shame. He watches you and knows how you move, what makes you tick, what you most desire, and what your inclinations and sensitivities are. He has a whole report on you for the purpose of knocking you down to prevent you from finishing your race.

In Genesis 3 we see the strategy of the serpent in action: "Now the serpent was more crafty than any of the wild animals the LORD God had made. He said to the woman, 'Did God really say, "You must not eat from any tree in the garden"?'" (Genesis 3:1).

The fact that satan used the body of a snake, which is described as crafty, is telling about the way he operates.

1. He is crafty.
2. He needs a vehicle to move through.

Crafty is defined as "clever at achieving one's aims by indirect or deceitful methods."[6] Similar words are *shrewd*, *cunning*, *tricky*, *sly*, and *sneaky*. Satan knows exactly who to use and what to use to slither into your world to bring you into the bondage of shame.

He used a snake with Eve, and he used my ex-boyfriend with me when he convinced me to continue living in sin at the cost of my intimacy with God. Sis, the enemy will use whoever and whatever he can to draw you away from God, and you'll find yourself naked and ashamed.

Shame was ushered into the human experience through the gratification of fleshly desires, and it tried to poison our relationship with God. But Paul gave us the antidote: "So I say, walk by the Spirit, and you will not gratify the desires of the flesh" (Galatians 5:16).

We must walk in the Spirit.

Walking in the Spirit

I wish I weren't this way, but your girl loves to overcomplicate things. I don't do it on purpose, but something inside me tends to think that if something is too simple or lacks complexity, then something is missing. If overthinking to death had a spokesperson, I'd be hired.

I remember one day when my daughter was about five, and she started acting up while we were out at dinner. She was doing the mostest with the hostess, and the anxiety building up in me was unexplainable. I just knew the people I was with thought I had no control over my kid and that I was a bad mother. My mind can lean toward the extreme side of things, and I was so overwhelmed by shame and embarrassment and the thought that people were judging me that I wanted to take my daughter into the bathroom and tell her she needed to get it together.

Anybody who was raised with parents who didn't spare the rod understands what a trip to the bathroom means when you're not at home. I was triggered. My daughter knew better. So why wasn't she behaving better? Here we were, simply trying to have a nice dinner and enjoy the company of the people we were with, but she decided to act up. And her acting up was making my feelings of shame and humiliation act up too. It wasn't a good look for me and my ego.

My mind started to chatter with what I wanted to say to my daughter. *Kamila, you know better than to interrupt*

136

adults while they are speaking. Girl, why are you acting like this even after I gave you the "look"? Have you lost your mind?

You may think my desire was to have a well-behaved, obedient, polite child, but that ain't the truth at all. My real desire was to be looked upon favorably by the people we were with, and as a result, I made a hasty trip to the bathroom, where I gave my daughter two spanks on her backside with the hope that compliance would soon follow.

In that moment my fear of the shame that would come from what people thought of me caused me to act a certain way. My friends didn't make me act the way I did; I made me act that way. It didn't just happen. I made a choice according to my flesh. I disciplined my daughter, not out of love but because of my shame.

Walking in the Spirit is no different. It's not something that automatically happens; it's something we have to choose to do every second of every day. We tend to overcomplicate this part of our journey as believers and think that walking in the Spirit requires us to do a bunch of things, but that's not the case. We must choose to do one thing.

Walking in the Spirit isn't about praying.

Walking in the Spirit isn't about reading your Bible.

Walking in the Spirit isn't about going to church.

Walking in the Spirit is *choosing* to walk in the new life of Jesus Christ. Paul explained it like this to the church of Ephesus:

So I tell you this, and insist on it in the Lord, that you must no longer live as the Gentiles do, in the futility of their thinking. They are darkened in their understanding and separated from the life of God because of the ignorance that is in them due to the hardening of their hearts. Having lost all sensitivity, they have given themselves over to sensuality so as to indulge in every kind of impurity, and they are full of greed. That, however, is not the way of life you learned when you heard about Christ and were taught in him in accordance with the truth that is in Jesus. You were taught, with regard to your former way of life, to put off your old self, which is being corrupted by its deceitful desires; to be made new in the attitude of your minds; and to put on the new self, created to be like God in true righteousness and holiness. (Ephesians 4:17–24)

We tend to think walking in the Spirit is all these things we *must* do, but no, it's simply making the choice to put off your old self and put on your new self. I hate to break it to you, but it is not that deep. Walking in the Spirit is trading in our dirty fig leaves from the garden for the new garments God made for us in love (Zechariah 3:4).

Now, please know that I'm not encouraging you to abandon spiritual disciplines. Praying, reading your Bible, and going to church are all fruits, the results of making the choice to walk in the Spirit. These spiritual disciplines are evidence of the spiritual choices we've made.

Remember the whole WWJD movement? WWJD stood for "What Would Jesus Do?" and people everywhere were wearing those colorful bracelets on their wrists to serve as a reminder to approach every situation and decision as Jesus would. They were telling the world that they had made a choice to follow Jesus, even when they were tempted not to. They were reppin' Jesus unashamedly. But reppin' Jesus is only part of how we walk in the Spirit; we must also operate in His power and strength—not our own.

Suit Up and Stand

Scripture tells us, "Finally, be strong in the Lord and in his mighty power. Put on the full armor of God, so that you can take your stand against the devil's schemes" (Ephesians 6:10–11).

Did you catch that? For us to take a stand against the schemes of the wicked one, we must stand in the power of God! Our only job is to suit up and stand.

Since we have been focusing on the senses and the role they play in the shame game, I am not going to go super deep into the full armor of God, but I do want to mention what it is because it's key to living shame-free.

To understand what Paul was talking about, it's important to understand the time in which his readers lived. Paul's readers were all subjects of the Roman Empire and would have been familiar with the appearance of Roman soldiers marching around in their full armor. He used the illustration of armor because the people saw this in their everyday life.

Though we may not be accustomed to seeing soldiers walking around in armor, the idea of war isn't foreign. A soldier isn't equipped to face battle without certain things to ensure his or her safety—offensively and defensively. Since we have already established that we are in a spiritual war against shame, it's important that we aren't caught unprepared on the battlefield. The armor we put on is spiritual and must be worn so that "when the day of evil comes, you may be able to stand your ground" (Ephesians 6:13).

Friend, it's not *if* evil comes but *when* evil comes. Will you be prepared?

Think about it like this: If you go on vacation to Hawaii, you don't pack earmuffs and UGG boots, right? No, you prepare for the weather in Hawaii and pack what you need for sunbathing on the beach. Likewise, there is a certain attire for this spiritual war we are in, and if we aren't dressed appropriately, it would be like walking around in the middle of Antarctica wearing flip-flops. We'd be unprepared and in danger when shame showed up fully suited in lies and accusations.

Stand firm then, with the belt of truth buckled around your waist, with the breastplate of righteousness in place, and with your feet fitted with the readiness that comes from the gospel of peace. In addition to all this, take up the shield of faith, with which you can extinguish all the flaming arrows of the evil one. Take the helmet of salvation and the sword of the Spirit, which is the word of God. (Ephesians 6:14–17)

For our discussion here I want to focus on one piece of the wardrobe: the helmet of salvation. Think about this: What is a helmet for? It protects your head, right? Well, when we put on this part of our armor, it declares that we are spiritually minded. With our helmets on we are no longer ruled by what we see, hear, taste, touch, and smell. We are governed by God's Word, and on His Word we meditate day and night (Psalm 1:2).

When our spiritual senses are activated, we see shame for what it truly is and we are protected from the devil's accusations, insinuations, and lies. To be led not by our physical senses, we must activate our spiritual senses and discern what is truly happening spiritually.

Are your spiritual eyes open?

I love the illustration in the book of 2 Kings when the prophet Elisha prayed for his servant to see spiritually. They were surrounded by their enemies and the servant was scared, but Elisha was cool, calm, and collected. See, Elisha had his helmet on. He was seeing things spiritually, which kept him in perfect peace. He told his servant, "Don't be afraid . . . Those who are with us are more than those who are with them" (6:16). He then prayed, "Open his eyes, LORD, so that he may see." And Scripture says, "Then the LORD opened the servant's eyes, and he looked and saw the hills full of horses and chariots of fire all around Elisha" (6:17).

Isn't that amazing? This is my prayer for you as well, that your spiritual eyes may be opened to see that there are more for you than against you and to see as God would have you see (Ephesians 1:18).

Feelings of shame are something that everyone with a pulse and five senses deals with, but the remedy to walking away from shame's power is the same for all of us. The sooner we discipline our senses to surrender to the Spirit, the better equipped we become to walk shame-free in the victory that is offered to us through Christ.

So let's open our spiritual eyes, put on the helmet of salvation, and start walking in the Spirit so that we will "receive forgiveness of sins and a place among those who are sanctified by faith in [Jesus]" (Acts 26:18 ESV).

Garden Prayer

Lord God, I need Your help to navigate my senses to be able to walk shame-free as You created me to live. Open my eyes to see the areas of shame in my life the way You see them so that I am not ignorant to the enemy's devices. I recognize that shame has had authority in my desires and cravings in this world, and I surrender these desires to Your Holy Spirit. You are what I want, and I ask Your forgiveness for the things I have placed above You. Teach me how to live out what Your Word says in Matthew: "Are you tired? Worn out? Burned out on religion? Come to me. Get away with me and you'll recover your life. I'll show you how to take a real rest. Walk with me and work with me—watch how I do it. Learn the unforced rhythms of grace. I won't lay anything heavy or ill-fitting on you. Keep company with me and you'll learn to live freely and lightly" [11:28–30 MSG].

I'm ready to walk with You. In Jesus' name I pray, amen.

⌐ SPEAKING FIRE INTO YOUR SENSES ¬

I declare that my God can and will guard me from the temptations of my desires by giving me the authority to resist the enemy [1 Corinthians 10:13; James 4:7]. I wholeheartedly trust Him to "create in me a pure heart" and to "renew a steadfast spirit within me" that aligns all my senses toward Him [Psalm 51:10].

Lies

Exposing Your Enemy

My parents divorced when I was four, and unlike the typical scenario that tends to play out in our culture, my two youngest sisters and I stayed with our dad instead of our mom. I was so young when they divorced that I don't really have any memories of my parents being together.

My dad was a provider who made sure my sisters and I were always taken care of, and he made it clear that our only responsibility as kids was to go to school and play sports. He was such a great dad when it came to providing for us and being present. Every morning he fed us breakfast before school, packed our lunches, and always included a handwritten note. There was never a night that we didn't have a homemade dinner ready and waiting for us.

My dad was an architectural engineer, and our home was always filled with plans, blueprints, and eraser scraps from his drafting board. I would watch him so intently as he drafted drawings for his next project. Sometimes he'd clean up the kitchen after dinner and then work well into the night after we girls were tucked in bed.

Daddy was also involved in the PTA at our school and even made us sweet treats to share with our friends on special occasions. Believe me when I say *everyone* loved Mr. Martin! He was the cool dad who always took time to play the game "hot hands" (aka "red tomato" or "the hand slap game") with the kids after school while other parents were in a constant state of rush.

Every soccer game, cheerleading competition, or swim meet, my daddy was there.

He was a man of few words, and looking back, I now understand that his method of showing me love was by being present in my life and providing for me. It would be many years before I could admit how empty my emotional tank was as his daughter. When you have a parent who is so present, so good, and so wonderful in one area, it's almost impossible to admit that it's not enough—especially when you're a young girl who only wants to please her daddy. I adored his presence, but I needed his words. I appreciated his sacrifices, but I longed for his emotional validation. I attached myself to his protection, but I craved his approval.

So I learned to study my dad's face and mannerisms as a barometer of whether he was pleased or displeased with me. He could correct me with the snap of a finger or just a look. The mere thought of my dad disapproving of me was enough to break me. In my attempt to make sense of my world as a young girl, I began believing the lie that what I did as a daughter would either reinforce or negate my relationship with my daddy. If I was helpful and good, I would get a smile that spread to my daddy's eyes and my little heart would soar. If I wasn't helpful or good, I wouldn't get the smile I needed so desperately from the person I depended on for my every need.

As a mother myself, I now see the way God designed men and women differently and equipped us with different strengths. While it may not be true for everyone, overall, I would say that women play the role of nurturer while men are firmer in their approach. My parents' divorce didn't just place my mom and dad in separate households; it also placed my nurturer and my provider at two different addresses.

The need for any sign of reassurance from my daddy created a lie in me that I was only lovable if I was "perfect," and any mistake would drive me into a deep pit of shame. I would try to be entertaining and funny for him and can very vividly remember being at the dinner table and racking my brain, thinking, *What can I say to make Daddy smile? What can I do to make Daddy happy?* I would recite the day's achievements and eagerly anticipate a reaction. The people pleaser I've told you about in previous chapters was born in those early days in the kitchen with my daddy. A nod of acknowledgment or the crack of a smile was enough to make me feel as if I could do no wrong. Without it, I crashed under the lie that I was less than and deserved nothing.

This lie carried into my teenage years, and I started to let my insecurities dictate the kind of relationships I could have. The narrative of shame in my mind was that I was unlovable and only worthy of love if I did something good that someone else noticed and responded to. I was afraid of messing up and would beat myself up mentally when I made a mistake or did something that didn't earn me the reward of someone's approval. The lies of shame that bombarded my mind convinced me I was never good enough and left me oppressed and dejected. I had no idea as a young woman how to find the truth of my daddy's love.

When my dad responded to my emotional needs with the stoic face he wore by default, my mind repeated familiar lies that convinced me again that my daddy's perceived anger and unhappiness were somehow my fault. As children we tend to see ourselves reflected in the faces of our parents, and the less emotion my daddy expressed, the more shame used my emotions to lie to me. I didn't have the language or understanding to admit that my emotional needs were not being met, but it didn't stop the narrative from forming in my mind that I was to blame for their being neglected. This untruth became the default storyline throughout my adolescent and young adult life and eventually the truth I believed more than any other truth. If there was a gap in any relationship, I was the cause. The relationship gap Adam and Eve felt with God after the enemy lied to them was exactly how I felt in those early, formative years after my parents divorced. Adam and Eve didn't know their shame could negate their relationship with God, because scripturally we learn that the first mention of shame in the Bible is to point out that God's creation had no relationship with it. Genesis 2:25 says, "Now the man and his wife were both naked, but they felt no shame" (NLT).

When God created humankind, it was very good. His perfect creation was without shame. There was no need for it. This biblical truth makes clear that God's original intent for humanity was to live 100 percent free in community with God and creation. Shame grows where truth is not present, so we must know certain truths to be able to live without shame. For instance, we must be aware of the truth about the enemy and how he works.

Know Your Enemy. Defeat Your Enemy.

Too often we see satan as a distant foe instead of an enemy who is waging war on our souls. If we don't know his true identity as God's enemy and what he's capable of, we won't see ourselves in a battle with him. Any war strategist will tell you that the enemy who is most dangerous is the enemy you know nothing about.

Twenty-five hundred years ago there was a Chinese general and military strategist named Sun Tzu. In his book, *The Art of War*, he wrote, "If you know the enemy and know yourself, you need not fear the result of a hundred battles. If you know yourself but not the enemy, for every victory gained you will also suffer a defeat. If you know neither the enemy nor yourself, you will succumb in every battle."[7]

While the wisdom of man is not what we hang our hats on as believers, these words from a man of war bring great insight to the importance of knowing oneself (our identity) and knowing the enemy who is out to destroy you.

Jesus described our enemy in this way: "He was a murderer from the beginning, and does not stand in the truth, because there is no truth in him. When he lies, he speaks out of his own character, for he is a liar and the father of lies" (John 8:44 ESV).

The lie the enemy has been whispering in the ears of God's children since the garden is the same lie that invites us to choose our own desires and our own will and to live off our own effort. He lied when he told Adam and Eve they would be better off going after what they wanted instead of living from what God had already provided. He lied when he enticed them to exercise their free will as though it would make them freer. The enemy lied then, and he still lies now.

When God removed the serpent from the garden after the fall, the serpent had access to see everything God intended for His creation but no right to possess any of it. And if he can't have it, he'll stop at nothing to make sure we can't have it. He parades in front of us all that we *could* have, but he uses our shame to convince us that we can't actually have it. He's not offering anything he created on his own. He's trying to resell God's promises by making one small change to God's invitation to us. He replaces God's "because" with his "if" and we never see it coming.

He says, *You will be if* . . .

God says, *You are because* . . .

When we can recognize the difference between what God and satan are saying, we won't settle for a knock-off promise because we already have the real thing. We won't go to war with an enemy for an inheritance we already possess. We won't believe the shaming lies of someone who lives outside of the truth.

Our first parents embraced the lies of the serpent because they didn't recognize that he was trying to get them to live alongside him in his choice to rebel. Adam and Eve had intimate fellowship with God. They could see, hear, and experience His tangible presence in and about their lives. In Eden, they heard His audible voice, sensed His actual footsteps, and spent one-on-one time with Him. God was not distant with His children; He was up close and personal with them. Their relationship lacked nothing. The serpent had enjoyed some of the same benefits in the garden until he'd longed for more. This was why he believed he had a shot at convincing Adam and Eve to long for more.

When the enemy spoke, suddenly Eve began to hear a new voice telling her what she *could* have and she forgot what she *already* had. This new conversation promised her more than what she was already given. The invitation to a new possibility made her lose sight of what God had already guaranteed. So she traded the truth for a lie. It wasn't that she didn't want God's truth, but maybe she didn't know how to process both a lie and a truth in the same space. The garden at this point had been a safe place for her without any threat or concern. Why wouldn't she believe this serpent was just as harmless as the worm Adam had just named? Lies are like that. They sneak up in the places we feel safe and protected and sucker punch us the same way the enemy's lie did Eve.

We often get judgmental and blame Eve for selling out in the garden, but let me make two things clear. One, Adam was right there with her, and he didn't know what to do with the truth and a lie in the same place any more than Eve did. Two, if we are honest, we have all been sucker punched by a lie and did not know how to respond. We've all felt safe in a place one moment and then deceived in the next. We like to think we'd respond differently, but the truth is we don't know how we would have responded in the garden. We have no idea what we would have remembered and what we would have forgotten. It wasn't that Eve didn't know better; it was that she forgot *the better*. She forgot that it was God her Creator, not a serpent, whose voice she should heed.

When was the last time you forgot to remember the truth when faced with a lie?

Can you think back to a time when you forgot what you *knew* when everything you knew changed because of a lie?

What happened to you when you forgot the promise because the place of promise no longer felt safe?

Since the beginning of time, the enemy's main shame tactic has been to amplify his half-truths to silence God's full truth. And the reality is, if you don't know the truth, the enemy has no problem feeding you his lies. This is why we must know the truth, remember the truth, and fight for the truth. It's only the truth that will set us free (John 8:32).

I'll never forget the day I found out the truth about what my daddy really believed about me. Even as I got older, I was still too terrified to communicate my emotional and personal needs out of fear of rejection or, even worse, silence. I don't think my daddy knew how

Since the beginning of time, the enemy's main shame tactic has been to amplify his half-truths to silence God's full truth.

truly alone I felt when I sat in his silence. So, one day, out of desperation, I decided to try something new. If I couldn't express my feelings verbally, maybe I could write them.

I wrote a letter that uncovered the parts of my heart I had learned to hide. I shared how scared I was that he was mad at me for not living up to the expectations he had set for me and the ones I had set for myself. In vulnerability I wrote down the countless times I had dropped the ball he didn't even know I was carrying. As I wrote each word, part of the shame from what had remained unspoken all those years weakened. I conveyed how deeply afraid I was that I would make a mistake that would cause him to give up on me or regret his hand in my life. I poured out every part of my heart in that letter without reservation, and yet I wholeheartedly believed and expected my words to be met with more silence.

I was wrong.

My father wrote back in his perfect penmanship that naturally slanted as though he were purposely italicizing every word. He opened the letter with these words:

Mariela,

You are such a blessing to me, and I am so proud of the young lady you are. There are very few things that you could do to upset me . . . so eliminate that thought.

I'll never forget those words because they set me free and overthrew the lies I had believed for so long. He poured out his love, approval, and affirmation over me, which began to dismantle the lie I had allowed to keep me hidden in shame. He reminded me of his immovable presence in my life and my unwavering position in his heart. His silence was not a reflection of something I had done wrong but a reflection of something he desperately wanted to get right yet didn't know how.

I still can't believe I had so vehemently believed a lie about my father that was shattered with just one honest letter. So many moments of shame and guilt played through my mind as I came to the full realization of how deeply rooted that lie was within me.

I wish I had learned sooner how to silence the lies instead of silencing the truth.

I wish I had given myself a chance to have an honest conversation with my dad instead of having so many lying conversations with the enemy.

I wish I would have responded the way Jesus did when He had an opportunity to have a truthful conversation.

Truthful Conversations

Luke 4 tells us about a wilderness moment that turned into an interesting conversation when Jesus had a run-in with satan and his lies. In case you forgot the story or don't know it, here's a fairy-tale version:

Once upon a time, Jesus was led into the wilderness by the Holy Spirit, and the devil showed up to have a conversation. He tried to sell Jesus three lies, and each time Jesus responded with a truth that had already been declared by His Father. Jesus didn't argue or negotiate what was being offered to Him. He just replied all three times with, "It is written . . ." After the third time, the devil left Him "until an opportune time," and the Lord sent angels to His Son to comfort and care for Him because He was hungry. (Luke 4:1–13)

Great little Sunday school story, right?

If we're not paying attention, we can gloss over parts of the Bible and write them off as good Christian stories and never take the time to see what these truthful conversations reveal to us today. The parallels in Jesus' encounter with the enemy and Adam and Eve's encounter with the same enemy reveal some hidden truths that help us get back to living shame-free. The first mention of the enemy ever speaking to humanity was in the garden, and the first mention of the enemy ever speaking to our Savior was in the wilderness.

Why are these conversations so important?

What do they teach us about our current conversations with shame?

It's important because of the biblical principle of the first mention.

Over and over again in Scripture, we see the blessing

and authority of the first mention. The law of first mention teaches that to understand a biblical principle in its original context, we have to go back to where that principle first appeared in Scripture. Once we understand the principle from the lens of the first mention, we can then use that first model to understand every other mention. Let's look at the first mention of the enemy and his lies from the law of the first mention.

In the garden Adam and Eve believed the first lie in the first conversation with the serpent, and we can clearly see how every generation thereafter continued in that model. That is, until Jesus showed us how to change the narrative of lies and shame. But before Jesus could speak to the lies of the enemy in the wilderness, God the Father had to deal with the first lie in the garden so the cycle of shame could be broken through His Son. Right before Jesus was led into the wilderness, we read about His baptism in the previous chapter (Luke 3). His baptism moment may not seem connected to His wilderness moment, but it is. Jesus' baptism was where God had to reestablish the first mention of His unconditional love and approval so that Jesus could change the narrative of the first mention of shame when He got to the wilderness.

The text reads, "And a voice came from heaven: 'You are my Son, whom I love; with you I am well pleased'" (Luke 3:22).

Now, we talked in chapter 4 about this moment being a declaration of approval and affirmation over Jesus, but now I want to show you something else about this pivotal moment. The approval God publicly declared is *what* happened at Jesus' baptism, but there's so much more to understanding *why* it happened. Jesus' baptism represented not only our fall in the garden, but more important, our resurrection in Him. What happened in the garden sank below the waves as Jesus was submerged, and all His unwavering promises to us came back up when He came up to the surface. In the depths of the Jordan, our shame drowned, and out of the water came the power and authority to respond differently to the enemy and his lies. And for the first time since the garden, nakedness without shame existed again as Jesus stood under an open heaven in the middle of the river. Let me explain what I mean.

I don't know for sure what Jesus was or wasn't wearing in the water that day, but I know His life was fully naked and vulnerable before the Father. He had stripped off His title and left His throne to restore our innocence (Galatians 4:3–5). He didn't just take off His robes of majesty and clothe Himself in the nakedness of humanity because He had nothing better *to do*. No, He had something better *to give*. The "better" He brought down from heaven was the truth that God's love liberates us from the enemy's lies and repositions us in our original position of authority and dominion alongside Him—but without the shame of the garden (1 Peter 3:21–22 AMP).

Through Jesus' work on the cross, we are united with

Him in His baptism, His resurrection, and His authority. Suddenly, the original plans and promises of God, which we thought were lost in the garden, became the plans and promises still available to us in Christ (Romans 5:17). Through the gospel, for the first time since shame popped up in Genesis, we have a real shot at living in the garden of provision and protection once again.

Okay, back to Jesus in the wilderness.

Right after God's public declaration over Jesus at His baptism, satan was desperate for the chance to contort God's words and make Jesus believe a lie. Since this wilderness encounter is the first mention of a conversation between Jesus and the devil, it provides us with a model for how to silence the enemy and the lies he spews.

Jesus didn't stay silent, as Adam did in the garden. As soon as He was presented with a lie, He responded with the voice of authority and truth rather than the absence and avoidance of truth. He wasn't tempted by the lies satan was offering. Nor was He tempted to doubt who His Father was or who He was in His Father's eyes. He wasn't played by the notion that His Father's provision was satan's to dole out. And He certainly felt qualified to tell the enemy to back the heck off. Jesus took advantage of that conversation, and the enemy had no choice but to shut up.

And the devil said to Him, "If You are the Son of God, command this stone to become bread."

But Jesus answered him, saying, "It is written, 'Man shall not live by bread alone, but by every word of God.'"

Then the devil, taking Him up on a high mountain, showed Him all the kingdoms of the world in a moment of time. And the devil said to Him, "All this authority I will give You, and their glory; for this has been delivered to me, and I give it to whomever I wish. Therefore, if You will worship before me, all will be Yours."

And Jesus answered and said to him, "Get behind Me, Satan! For it is written, 'You shall worship the LORD your God, and Him only you shall serve.'"

Then he brought Him to Jerusalem, set Him on the pinnacle of the temple, and said to Him, "If You are the Son of God, throw Yourself down from here. For it is written:

'He shall give His angels charge over you,
To keep you.'

and,

'In their hands they shall bear you up,
Lest you dash your foot against a stone.'"

And Jesus answered and said to him, "It has been said, 'You shall not tempt the LORD your God.'"

(Luke 4:3–12 NKJV)

For far too long we have believed the lies of the enemy and succumbed to the pattern and narrative of Adam and Eve when it comes to conversations with the enemy, but Jesus invites us to respond His way. His model in the wilderness is one of truthfulness filled with confidence, restoration, and redemption—a stark contrast to Adam and Eve's model. When it comes to battling and prevailing over your enemy, avoidance isn't healing and silence isn't golden. We can now overturn the enemy's lies by forcing a truthful conversation that changes the narrative from shame to authority, regret to identity, and guilt to security.

> **When it comes to battling and prevailing over your enemy, avoidance isn't healing and silence isn't golden.**

A New Narrative

You may be wondering, *How do I silence the lies?* That's the million-dollar question, right?

The short answer: be like Jesus.

To silence the enemy's lies, you and I need to follow the same model Jesus did in the wilderness. When you speak about God's greater authority over him, his lies have no life in them. When you take a stand against the temptations the enemy offers, his position in your life changes from tormentor to tormented. When you remind him what the Bible says about who we are—children of God (1 John 3:1–2)—his voice is silenced. You are free—shame-free—and you can take hold of the promise that there is not a single verse in any translation that echoes the lies he tries to feed you. In fact, every scripture contradicts his lies. Let's build an "it is written" list for you so that when the enemy tries to come for you in your wilderness, you'll know exactly how to respond.

It is written:

And you will know the truth, and the truth will set you free. (John 8:32 NLT)

And so we know and rely on the love God has for us. God is love. Whoever lives in love lives in God, and God in them. (1 John 4:16)

Therefore, there is now no condemnation for those who are in Christ Jesus. (Romans 8:1)

Yet in all these things we are more than conquerors through Him who loved us. For I am persuaded that neither death nor life, nor angels nor principalities nor powers, nor things present nor things to come, nor height nor depth, nor any other created thing, shall be able to separate us from the love of God which is in Christ Jesus our Lord. (Romans 8:37–39 NKJV)

Now the salvation and the power and the kingdom of our God and the authority of his Christ have come, for the accuser of our brothers has been thrown down, who accuses them day and night before our God. (Revelation 12:10 ESV)

Your accuser of shame has been thrown down.

He's done. He's defeated. His voice has no power. His narrative has been silenced.

Let me show you in the garden where God did this.

We know God moved Adam and Eve out of the garden out of love, not punishment, so they wouldn't eat from the tree of eternal life and live with guilt and shame for eternity. But did we also connect that God moved them out of the garden so they could be a billboard of His grace to the enemy all the days of their lives? See, Adam and Eve couldn't remind the enemy on a daily basis of his defeat in the garden because God had banished him from there. While the enemy wandered outside the garden, so did Adam and Eve, reminding him of his defeat. Their lives followed him and served as a megaphone of God's redemption over them. Adam and Eve may have been on the outside of the garden, but they weren't outside of their relationship with God. God not only removed Adam and Eve to save them from an eternity of shame, but He also positioned them to declare loudly that the enemy hadn't won. And in doing so, God showed us how to silence the enemy's voice for all the things we've done in the past and for all the future things we'll do that the enemy is waiting to accuse us of later.

You and I are free, and it's not because of what we've done but because of what Jesus has done. The longer you linger in what is written in His Word about you, the more what you *know* becomes what you *believe*. Once we wholeheartedly believe His truth, we can recognize someone else's lies and call them out instead of just accepting them as truth. We take the narrative away from the enemy and put it back in the mouth of our God.

God's love plucks away every shameful thought that doesn't align with His truth until all we're left with is the truth that remains—His truth and no one else's. Just like the miracle of the letters my dad and I exchanged. After I fully embraced the new truth that my daddy was telling me, I could eliminate the contrary thoughts, the negative thoughts, and the lies about who I was to him. I was deeply loved by my daddy and no lie from the enemy could take that away—even the ones I'd rehearsed and replayed in my mind more times than I could count.

After reading my story, I pray you feel the need to write a letter as well. Maybe you feel the need to write a letter to God telling Him all the lies you've been believing. Or perhaps you sense the need to write a letter to your parents, spouse, or kids to expose all the untruths that have become your truths for far too long. You may even feel the pull to write a letter to yourself to see the truth for the first time.

Take me up on this, friend—write that letter.

If you're worried about who will write you back, don't trip. God already covered that. He's already written back. How? In His Word. The Bible has been called a sixty-six-book love letter—each chapter written to us. Each book expresses His love for us in some way, and we can go back and read it as many times as we need to. You might be surprised by what you read without the background noise of shame in your head.

That's how it was for me when I read my daddy's letter and that's how I pray it is for you as you read your heavenly Daddy's letter to you.

Garden Meditation

Let the narratives of today fall away as you begin an honest conversation with God. Maybe it's been a long time since you've really talked to God and allowed Him to speak truth into the lies you've carried. This is your moment. Let Him speak over you the promises He's written for you, and make a conscious choice to believe Him. As you listen and speak, ask Him to show you

- the lying, shameful narratives the enemy has been playing over and over in your mind and heart and how to stop them once and for all;
- which truthful conversations you need to have to begin dismantling the enemy's lies; and
- His love letter written in His Word. Start by reading Psalm 139.

⌐ SPEAKING FIRE TO EXPOSE THE LIES ¬

I declare that I will be guided in God's truth and no longer allow the deceit of the enemy to speak a contrary word into my spirit [Psalm 25:5; John 8:32]. I refuse to believe half-truths that are outside of His Word, His will, and His plan for my life [John 16:13]. I choose to live with my eyes and heart open and vulnerable as evidence of my complete surrender and belief in Him as the way, the truth, and the life [John 14:1, 6].

GARDEN
LESSON
Eight

Nakedness

Silencing Shame

When my parents divorced, my relationship with my mom was loving but detached. I had her, but I didn't *have* her. She lived at another address, and she wasn't part of my daily life. I visited her as much as I could and loved those summers with her, but I was very aware that I was being raised in a single-parent home. I learned to adapt to being raised solely by a male, and because my daddy's physical presence was so amazing, I don't think I necessarily missed having a mom as a young girl. But looking back as a mom myself now, I can see where I developed a roughness around my edges. I understand now why I was more comfortable being a tomboy who steered away from makeup and dresses and had more guy friends than female friends. I never seemed to feel comfortable around girls, and even as an adult, I never was the girl with a long list of girlfriends. But as I got older, something in me yearned for close friends like that.

The reality was, I wasn't really in touch with my femininity because I didn't have any experience or real, consistent exposure to it. My mom and I talked throughout my life, but it was always more catch-up than connection. In fact, I didn't really feel that I needed or wanted a mom. I felt like that ship had sailed and I was good on my own without a close bond with my mom. I didn't see my rough-and-tough demeanor as an entire outfit of fig leaves, but I also knew I wasn't really naked with the whole mom conversation either. Isn't it just like God to use circumstances to show us areas that are still covered up?

About five years ago, my mom was without her new husband and without a home. She was divorcing the man she'd married on my fourteenth birthday, she was moving out, and the nephew she'd raised was going off to college, leaving her alone. She didn't like that idea, and suddenly I was faced with the real possibility of living with my mom again after being separate for over three decades. *Um, what are You doing, God?*

After much contemplation and prayer, I decided that my mom could move into the granny flat we had downstairs.

Again, God, um . . . what? The day I had prayed for during my childhood was coming to pass so many years later when I had children of my own. For the first time, I had my mom.

It was a lot to take in, and I went through a range of emotions daily. As we learned to occupy the same space more like strangers than mom and daughter, I learned she talked a lot and always wanted to ask me all the things all the time. I would think to myself, *Do all women talk this much?* Being raised in silence with my dad taught me to be comfortable in quietness and actually prefer it; it was what I was accustomed to. My mom was anything but quiet for about 90 percent of the day. She would ask me questions I would *never* think to ask anyone, and I often wondered what my life would have been like if I'd come home every day to someone who was as interested in my emotions, my day, and my thoughts as she was now.

I studied how she kept to herself and her space when she wasn't talking, and I started learning things I didn't know and was never taught—like how to move in gentleness and patience toward your child. I struggled with this with my own children, especially when I was so harsh and critical toward myself. She was gentle, kind, and nurturing, and to be honest, it made me pretty uncomfortable. Most of the time, it was too much attention for me, too much serving me, too much loving on me, and just too much availability for me. I wasn't used to that, but I slowly let myself be naked before her and I realized God had given me my mom at a time I needed her most.

He brought her into my life so I could feel what it was like to be truly seen, known, and loved unconditionally not just by God, but within a relationship I didn't even know I needed and wanted so deeply. Time with her allowed me to see her nakedness as well as to help heal the shame she felt for not being present in our lives. She could be seen, known, and loved by the daughter she thought she had lost.

Together, we learned how to stand without shame from the past, naked in our need, naked in our love, naked in our forgiveness. It didn't happen in an instant, but it did happen, and it's still happening today.

The reason I could accept and celebrate the journey of healing with my mom was because I had already been on a journey with God's Garden Lessons. Learning to battle shame, reignite my faith, and reclaim my purpose wasn't an overnight victory but a day-to-day process of following Him until my baby steps led me to healing and reclaiming. It was a process I trusted with God, so I knew I could trust it for my relationship with my mom. Neither journey of restoration was a magical fairy tale of doing all the right things at all the right times. Instead, both relationships—mine with God and mine with my mom—were made up of daily decisions to live naked while choosing to put on new garments of freedom God had for me each morning.

It's been a journey that has been difficult at times

because of me, and yet also easy because of Him (Matthew 11:30). I've walked in strength in establishing boundaries, and I've walked in fear that I would always crave approval. I've stepped into the right choices with the Spirit, and I've stepped into the wrong ones with my flesh. There have been moments defined by breakthroughs in my purpose, and there have been moments defined by breakdowns in my identity. Sometimes I went to bed knowing I had made progress exposing the enemy's lies, and sometimes I cried myself to sleep in disappointment of old rhythms I couldn't shake.

What has been my greatest takeaway through it all?

Every hill and every valley have been part of the journey, part of the story, and part of God's purpose for my life.

It was this revelation of freedom in the *journey* rather than in the *destination* that allowed me to stay naked throughout the learning process. I let people see me walk through identity, purpose, community, approval, boundaries, senses, and lies, and it was liberating in ways I never could have imagined. I shared my steps through She Speaks Fire, regardless of whether those steps were perfect, neat, or presentable. I welcomed anyone who wanted to hear how I was succeeding and failing as a wife, mom, and Christian. I chased nothing but truth and transparency, and God started to show me that naked living is favored living. Conversations, opportunities, and connections started coming after me instead of me having to chase them down. Everything I wasn't looking for came looking for me.

I chased nothing but truth and transparency, and God started to show me that naked living is favored living.

Still, shame kept trying to show up to my freedom party, begging me to wear its fig leaves again.

Although I didn't give in, shame's voice and presence tried to convince me that I hadn't changed at all by tempting me to revert to approval addiction, identity crisis, or isolation from community. The enemy's new lie was that the mere fact that shame kept showing up, looking for a seat at the table, was proof that I was still inviting it into my life. But the truth is, even though shame showed up uninvited in my mind, its seat in my spirit was no longer empty. Jesus had taken that seat, and He gave shame the boot every time it showed up.

Shame isn't something we will ever conquer until heaven, but it can be silenced here on earth (Psalm 143:12). We press the Mute button on shame when we sit confidently in our seat next to Jesus while intentionally guarding our hearts so that shame knows it isn't welcome to stay and get cozy again. Oh, I know it may be lingering at my door, hoping I'll cover up again and give it a voice in my life, but I also know its showing up doesn't mean I have to give up my freedom and my shame-free nakedness. And neither do you.

There are steps we can take to keep our souls and spirits naked before God, ourselves, and others to ensure our freedom isn't fleeting. To make it simple, I've come up with three steps we must take to battle shame and reignite our faith. My hope is that you'll read these three things for the first time to get it and for the hundredth time to keep it.

Step 1: Remain Vulnerable

The first thing to go when shame entered the garden was vulnerability, and today, we must go to war to bring it back and keep it. Adam and Eve were completely vulnerable with each other in their nakedness before God, and it extended beyond a physical nakedness. Their vulnerability allowed them to hear the love of God without fear, see God without guilt, and respond to God without shame. But shame changed how they heard, what they saw, and how they responded the minute their eyes were uncovered. That change in vulnerability is what we're still trying to un-change to this day.

To be vulnerable means to be seen for who we really are, naked and flawed. It is to be honest about the fact that the only reason our naked humanity doesn't bring us shame any longer is because of God's goodness. A perfect example of this is the call for vulnerability and nakedness of the barren woman whom the Lord told to sing instead of hiding her shame, her infertility. While Isaiah 54 was originally written as a prophecy about the return of Israel from the Babylonian exile, its metaphorical treatment of Zion as a barren woman tells us a lot about vulnerability:

> "Sing, barren woman, you who never bore a
>   child;
> burst into song, shout for joy, you who were
>   never in labor;
> because more are the children of the desolate
>   woman than of her who has a husband. . . .
> "Do not be afraid; you will not be put to shame.
> Do not fear disgrace; you will not be humiliated.
> You will forget the shame of your youth
> and remember no more the reproach of your
>   widowhood."
>
>   (Isaiah 54:1, 4)

In modern language, the Lord is saying:

> Sing, you who struggle with depression, anxiety,
>   lust, or loneliness.
> Burst into song and shout for joy, you who are
>   battling disease, sickness, and doubt.
> Because more are the promises for those who
>   stay naked than for those who cower behind
>   shame.
> Do not be afraid; you will not be put to shame.
> Do not fear disgrace; you will not be humiliated.

You will forget the shame of your youth
and remember no more the pain and
   disappointment of what left you alone and
   grieving.

This biblical imagery of vulnerability is the true definition of *naked* and the freedom from shame our Lord offers.

When I look back at my own journey through the Garden Lessons of Genesis, it was vulnerability and honesty about where I was in life that silenced the shame I was carrying. I was able to be seen in the raw moments when I stood naked in front of God and those He sent to help me with my feelings of overwhelm, brokenness, anxiety, depression, and suffering.

How about you? Where are you with this conversation about being and remaining vulnerable?

Are you comfortable talking about your victories but never your failures?

Is it simply too much nakedness for you to be real about your struggles, so you'd rather suffer under the weight of imperfection?

We all have placed unrealistic expectations on what it means to be a Christian, which only feeds the cycle of shame because we are trying to outdo one another to be accepted. The transparent culture of She Speaks Fire has shown me that when we fight for vulnerability, we create a safe space to be honest about where we are and, as a result, give each other an opportunity to aid in the areas in which we are struggling. Without vulnerability we put pressure on others to preserve an image and "look the part" until we lose touch with what it is to live naked without any fig leaves in this fallen world.

Truth is, we all fall short (Romans 3:23). We all struggle, which keeps us at the foot of the cross, fully aware of our need for Jesus. Weakness does not make us powerless; it makes us constantly aware of the God who is all-powerful (2 Corinthians 12:9–10).

The sooner we realize that we all have weaknesses, the sooner we can silence shame.

Now, I know you may be fighting me as you read. And I genuinely understand your resistance to vulnerability. When we are vulnerable, we open ourselves up to potentially be wounded as we share the rawest part of ourselves and our humanity. I understand baring your soul through vulnerability is easier said than done. I'm also aware that you may have tried that before and it resulted in rejection, silence, shock, or even apathy, which has deterred you and discouraged you from wanting to be open again. But you must fight to stay tender because of this promise from our God: "A bruised reed he will not break, and a smoldering wick he will not snuff out" (Isaiah 42:3).

My heart empathizes with you if you have had a negative experience with vulnerability that left you bruised and burned-out when your transparency revealed superficial relationships rather than deep ones. Today you may feel as if life in your community is nice, but there are no real, authentic, and honest connections. Maybe you need to ask yourself whether other people are the problem or you are, because you refuse to allow yourself to be open and vulnerable again.

Let me ask you the same question God asked me: *If you're already vulnerable before Me, why does it even matter if you're vulnerable before man?*

That's an honest question, right?

The Bible gives us clear direction in James 5:16 to confess our sins to one another so that we can be healed. In the same way God said it wasn't good for man to be alone in the garden, God also says it's not good for us to be alone in our struggle. God is fully aware that we will struggle, but He gave us both His Spirit and His people to help us carry our burdens (Galatians 6:2). And when He sees us operating in the power of unity that He originated in the garden between Himself and humanity, He sees it is good.

It doesn't seem as if it should be so hard for us to handle each other's nakedness, but aren't we all guilty of exposing one another's vulnerability rather than covering it? I've learned to know better than to throw the first stone at someone else's vulnerability because I am fully aware of my own vulnerability (John 8:7). I fight every day to live from a posture of nakedness, which means I'm choosing to live in a house of glass. And I'm okay with that because my glass windows don't just allow you to look in and see me; they also allow me to look out and see the sun, the stars, and the promise that I don't have to be afraid anymore.

I want to encourage you to take the first brave step to be vulnerable and show your weakness to someone. Call them. Text them. Let someone in, and allow that person to show you his or her weakness as well. You've been in the dark, carrying a burden on your back for too long. You've been crying yourself to sleep for too many nights. You've been hiding in the bushes with your sin for too many days. No more hiding. It's time to be vulnerable to get free and stay free, my friend.

Step 2: Release Fear and Rejection

Vulnerability is only step one. Pushing forward to release fear and rejection is the next essential step to remaining free. Fear is motivated by our instinctual senses that react when we feel we're in danger. Faith, on the other hand, is motivated by our response to the Spirit and His response to us. As believers, we can choose faith or fear, but we can't choose both. The Bible says, "There is no fear in love. But perfect love drives out fear, because fear has to do with punishment. The one who fears is not made perfect in love" (1 John 4:18).

It is by faith that we combat fear.

It is by God's perfect love that we overcome fear.

It is through the union of faith and love that we free ourselves from the power fear once had.

My biggest fear used to be rejection, and it caused me to do some questionable things over the years. Fear of disappointing people would paralyze me into agreeing to things I didn't really want to do and keep me silent when I wanted to speak. This was the case for so many years of my life until I decided enough was enough.

I realized I had a choice. Someone is always going to have something to say about me, and I can either live afraid because of that, or I can live free because of Christ. Isn't that true for all of us? Someone is always going to have an opinion about how you or I should do things, but *we can't please everyone.*

One of the biggest problems that comes from fearing people is that our fear places their applause higher than God's voice in our lives. Their opinions mean more to us than obedience to God, and they stand in the way of walking naked and free in our purpose. That's what happened in the garden and that's what's still happening with some of us today. The words "fear not" appear over and over in Scripture, but the verse that liberated me is in the book of Proverbs: "The fear of man lays a snare, but whoever trusts in the LORD is safe" (29:25 ESV).

Let's break that down. Scripture tells us that fearing people is a trap. A snare is what hunters set out to catch their prey, and when we fear people, we are walking straight into a trap set by the enemy himself.

So what is the answer? How do we avoid the snare? The latter part of that verse tells us how—by trusting in the Lord!

Trusting in the Lord is more than just putting our faith in who He says He is.

It's more than putting our faith in what He has promised to do.

It's trusting Him about who He says *we* are!

You are who God says you are. Period.

So who does He say you are?

In Him

you are a new creation (2 Corinthians 5:17),

you are chosen by God (Ephesians 1:11),

you are forgiven and redeemed (Ephesians 1:7),

you are holy and blameless (Ephesians 1:4), and

you are kept in safety wherever you go (Psalm 91:11).

You are not who *you* say you are and you're not who *someone else* says you are. You're God's. He created you, named you, and rebuilt what shame tried to destroy in you so that you could finally release the fear and rejection you've been holding.

My prayer for you is that fear no longer rules you. I pray that you stop allowing people's opinions to dictate your life. I pray you see yourself as a narrative of redemption instead of a narrative of shame. I pray that you see that the enemy and his three weapons—shame, fear, and rejection—have no power in your life.

What are practical ways this plays out in our everyday lives?

Spend time with God. Get direction and go—even if that's

outside the safety and comfort of your garden. God's direction breaks the bondage of fear and rejection and always moves us in the direction of His unwavering purpose. After all, if He is for you, then who can be against you (Romans 8:31)?

When you stop fearing people, you bring confidence to your spirit and speak with fire to your fig leaves, "The Lord is my helper; I will not fear; what can man do to me?" (Hebrews 13:6 ESV). As you spend time with Him and in His Word, you will naturally begin to

> trust that God is your vindicator and your protector (Psalm 57:2–3),
>
> trust that He is leading and guiding you into all truth (John 16:13),
>
> trust that no weapon formed against you can prosper—even the weapons of people's opinions (Isaiah 54:17 NKJV),
>
> trust that greater is He who is in you than he who is in the world (1 John 4:4),
>
> trust that you are free from the fear and rejection of people because you are no longer a slave to man or to fear (Romans 8:15), and
>
> trust that you are God's and a servant of Christ (Galatians 1:10).

Trusting in God releases fear and rejection so that you can silence shame. God is with you and so am I. Let my prayers over you remind you there is someone talking to God about you and cheering you on as you allow the Garden Lessons to teach you repeatedly, so that shame never speaks louder than God and His Word again.

I want to pause here to say that I have a special heart for moms, especially single moms, trying to live without shame. Let me pray this over you today:

Lord, I pray for fear to be broken over the life of Your daughter. I pray that Your voice becomes stronger in her life and that truth becomes louder than any lie coming against her or her children. I pray that You free the heart of this mom from the need for approval that has kept her stuck. I pray that You give her back her voice so she can embrace with open arms all that You have called her to be. Put people in her life who will uplift her, support her, and speak truth into her life and the lives of her children. Today, I declare freedom over each single mom so that they may share their story with fire and freedom for someone else. In Jesus' name, amen.

Step 3: Rest in Grace

After we move in vulnerability and release fear and rejection, we must learn how to rest in His grace. Sin in the garden exchanged reliance on God as the primary provider for reliance on our own ability to meet our needs (Genesis 3:17–19). But when we are born into Christ, salvation is exchanged again from self-reliance with a much greater governing principle: grace. Scripture says, "And if by grace, then it cannot be based on works; if it were, grace would no longer be grace" (Romans 11:6).

In grace we no longer depend on ourselves to make things happen, but instead depend again on the indwelling life of Christ and enter into His rest. Outside of grace, rest isn't the priority, running is. Instead of rest and freedom, we find ourselves running on a hamster wheel of labor and performance, trying to attain something that has already been attained in Christ.

I used to think working and striving was my portion in life. It didn't matter if I was talking about marriage, parenting, career, or ministry. If I was in it, then I was running and striving for it. I wanted to prove I had what it took to be successful, but the whole game changed when I stopped trying to prove my worth and just started operating from it. I didn't need to prove to people that my life was healed for it to be healed. I stopped listening to the voice inside me that said I had to work more, stay later, drive harder, and be better to show that I was capable of living in the fullness of God's purpose. Too many of us still live under this old governing belief where we're always striving toward becoming something we already are. We are constantly on the hunt to find that which is already ours. We find ourselves begging God to do something He has already done. And guess what? We're left feeling ashamed that we are asking for too much while not doing enough.

You might be saying, "Sis, I want to rest, but I *can't* rest. If I rest, these kids won't eat, my family won't have clean clothes, and these bills won't get paid." I get it. I really do. But the rest I'm talking about isn't focused only on stopping (although sometimes you do just need to stop); it's a rest that's focused on pauses and peace. The biblical king best known for wisdom, King Solomon, said, "One hand full of rest and patience is better than two fists full of labor and chasing after the wind" (Ecclesiastes 4:6 AMP).

Listen to the wisdom in that verse: it's "better" to keep one hand on rest than two hands on work. I believe God is trying to tell us that when we work, we need to work from a posture of rest rather than striving. He wants us to work in such a way that we *can* stop or pause to rest when we need to.

You may think I'm making resting in Him sound like an easy thing to do, but when all you've done is run through your life, I know how hard it is to stop and rest. The ability to stop racing from task to task requires peace in your spirit and trust in your soul. Remember, one of the main reasons Jesus came was to give us rest and freedom because living in a perpetual state of proving ourselves robs us of rest (Matthew 11:28). God wants us to slow down, operate from peace, and start living and resting in grace. It's in the resting that we take the third step toward staying free.

So now the pressure is off! We are *free*.

You can live contrary to the culture and the world system around you that says the more you move, the more you get rewarded. God's grace isn't a system at all, nor is it reflective of everything we've become accustomed to hearing. This is because resting and remaining in Him has an entirely different language than it does in the world.

The world says rest is for the weak.

Grace says He gives rest *to* the weak (Matthew 11:29).

The world says rest makes you too lazy to work.

Grace says rest gives you blessings that working can't (Psalm 127:2 AMP).

The world says rest opens the door for someone to take what you could have had.

Grace says rest silences the lie that anyone can take what God has already given you (Proverbs 1:33).

We must start seeing rest the way God sees it if we're going to stay free and not be weighed down by shame and other besetting sins. Genesis teaches us that rest was as much a part of the creation story as the actual creating (2:2–3). If God stopped and rested, why do we think we don't need to stop and rest too? It's not just an Old Testament thing either. The New Testament reiterates God's command to follow His model of rest in Hebrews: "There remains, then, a Sabbath-rest for the people of God; for anyone who enters God's rest also rests from their works, just as God did from his. Let us, therefore, make every effort to enter that rest, so that no one will perish by following [Israel's] example of disobedience" (4:9–11).

When we stop trying to do stuff for God and simply rest in Him as Adam and Eve did before the earth became cursed through sin, we align ourselves with His original model of rest and freedom. In our alignment we find our ordained work instead of our obligated work. We can be like Adam and Eve, who didn't have to strive in the garden. God ordained the work they were given to do, and He does the same for us. The ordained work of God gives us time to rest, but the obligated work of the world allows little or no time for rest. When you can separate the two, you can step out of obligated work and into ordained work.

You need rest, you deserve rest, and you can't skip this step.

Now What? New Garden, New Lessons

Is staying free as easy as three steps? Yes and no. Yes, it's easy because God isn't trying to trick you with an elaborate plan that has more for you to do. No, because these three steps aren't done in a moment. They happen over a lifetime of walking with the Lord. Walking away from shame isn't a quick fix; it's a journey of discovering and rediscovering the God who defeated it at the cross. Some Garden Lessons will keep you at step one for weeks as you learn the unforced rhythms of grace and freedom. Other Garden Lessons will keep you at step three for months or even years as you learn to let God sustain you in His rest. The beauty is that God isn't at the finish line of your life, just waiting for you to hurry up and get there.

He's at mile 1 with you, cheering you on as you start the learning and relearning process.

He's at mile 34 with you, carrying you to mile 35.

He's at mile 72 with you, coaching you on how to keep going another 25.

He's at every mile with you making sure you make it to the end—*without shame.*

If you can let yourself walk through these steps with Him, you will find and keep His freedom.

As you walk through the gardens of your life, stay vulnerable. Silence fear and rejection. Rest in God's grace.

Again, I'm not saying this is an easy process. I'm telling you it's possible.

And I'm telling you, you already have what you need inside you to live without shame.

At the end of *The Wizard of Oz*, Glenda, the Good Witch of the North, helps Dorothy discover that the way to get back

I'm telling you, you already have what you need inside you to live without shame.

home to Kansas was always within her. But before she could tap those ruby slippers three times, she had to figure out that she didn't really need a wizard to get back home. She had everything she needed already inside her. Her beloved friends, the Scarecrow, the Lion, and the Tin Man, wished they could have figured it out for her, but she never would have believed them. Freedom is like that. Others can wish it for you, want it for you, hope it for you, but only you can discover it and learn it for yourself.

You may not have had to learn it in Oz, but you had to learn it in the garden.

You learned how to battle shame.

You learned how to reignite your faith.

You learned how to reclaim your purpose.

You learned how to receive freedom in the finished work of Christ.

And everything you need to stay free is already in you.

You're ready because you're *free*.

There are books you will read once and put away on a shelf. I hope this isn't that kind of book for you. The life in this book comes from the truths that stay true for generations to come. Someone in your life is battling shame, and she needs what you have learned. She needs help uncovering what you let God uncover in these chapters. Someone else in your life is hiding behind his fig leaves, and he needs your help to get free. They both need the truth about shame that you have uncovered.

The best way you help these folks get free is by staying free. Don't let this book collect dust where God gave you hope. Don't let the change you unraveled in the chapters be forgotten. Don't close this book and close your heart. Come back to these pages and find your victory over shame again and again. It's okay to need the words on these pages again in the future. Let's be honest enough to admit we're all still works in progress until we get to heaven, knowing that Jesus' words still give us hope today: "In the world you have tribulation and trials and distress and frustration; but be of good cheer [take courage; be confident, certain, undaunted]! For I have overcome the world. [I have deprived it of power to harm you and have conquered it for you]" (John 16:33 AMPC).

Your life has fire in its DNA, and what comes from you will birth fire. Be true to who God created you to be, and keep coming back to the place in your own garden where you first heard the call and answered it. You can trust it. You can rely on it. You can rest in it.

Some days it may feel scary to live without your fig leaves, but going back to the things that shamed you is just as scary. You must choose your scary. I could tell you I'm never scared when I speak the fire within me, but that's a lie. I was scared starting my ministry and I was scared writing this book, but I was more scared of staying in my shame and not busting the move God told me to make. There were and are souls attached to my obedience, and there are souls attached to yours.

God created you for a reason, and your experience of

shame in the garden of your life cannot change that. The world is waiting for you to come out of hiding so you can speak fire without shame. It's time to let Him move you from your past into all that He has for you in the future. These Garden Lessons have helped you get this far, but now you must step out and walk this thing for yourself.

Let me tell you one last time . . .

No more shame.

No more hiding.

No more lies.

You're *free*—free to be and free to go.

So go, and may fire go before you as you find the fire within you.

Garden Reflection

Who were you when you started this journey through the garden? What has changed? What is the same? As you consider the Garden Lessons you've learned and are still learning, reflect on each one and begin to journal how each lesson helped you battle shame, reignite your faith, and reclaim your purpose.

- **Identity**
  - What has God taught me about battling shame?
  - Where has God reignited my faith?
  - How has God helped me reclaim my purpose?

- **Purpose**
  - What has God taught me about battling shame?
  - Where has God reignited my faith?
  - How has God helped me reclaim my purpose?
- **Community**
  - What has God taught me about battling shame?
  - Where has God reignited my faith?
  - How has God helped me reclaim my purpose?
- **Approval**
  - What has God taught me about battling shame?
  - Where has God reignited my faith?
  - How has God helped me reclaim my purpose?
- **Boundaries**
  - What has God taught me about battling shame?
  - Where has God reignited my faith?
  - How has God helped me reclaim my purpose?
- **Senses**
  - What has God taught me about battling shame?
  - Where has God reignited my faith?
  - How has God helped me reclaim my purpose?
- **Lies**
  - What has God taught me about battling shame?
  - Where has God reignited my faith?
  - How has God helped me reclaim my purpose?
- **Nakedness**
  - What has God taught me about battling shame?
  - Where has God reignited my faith?
  - How has God helped me reclaim my purpose?

SPEAKING FIRE TO LIVE NAKED AND FREE

I declare I am free and free indeed because the finished work of Christ has liberated my soul from shame [John 8:36]. I will come boldly to His throne every day, confident I will receive mercy and help on this journey of freedom [Hebrews 4:16]. I will not worry. I will not doubt. I will not live in shame. I will trust in my God, knowing He has never failed me, and He never will [Deuteronomy 31:8].

A Final Word

Speaking Fire

I specifically remember having a conversation with two women from my church who were afraid to share their stories out of fear that people would look at them differently. They were both exotic dancers who'd been set free by the blood of the Lamb, but they both carried so much shame about the lives from which God had rescued them. Shame had broken them down so deeply that they believed their lives were unredeemable.

I had a conversation with another woman who was afraid to speak about being delivered from same-sex attraction out of fear that people would judge her and shame her publicly. Her story was covered in fig leaves, and she never imagined being able to speak openly about what God had delivered her from.

You probably know countless similar stories from people

who have made a vow to keep their secrets hidden, even if they have experienced healing and redemption. Maybe you're one of them. Often, it's hard enough to accept your own story, but it's a thousand times more difficult to entrust that same story to others. However, the revelation of the Garden Lessons is that God wants to take you from silent shame to speaking fire.

The revelation of the Garden Lessons is that God wants to take you from silent shame to speaking fire.

I want to share with you something I posted on Instagram along with a picture of my daughter on her birthday:

I remember when I was a really bad mom. I remember when I was so broken and craved love so bad that I would leave my baby girl with a sitter for days at a time so I could be out in them streets. I remember choosing my boyfriend over time with her. I remember choosing partying over time with her. I remember choosing getting high over time with her. I was chasing love. I was chasing validation. I was chasing anything that would make me feel complete because I felt so empty. It makes me so sad to think how lonely she must have felt to have a shell of a mother who didn't know how to love her properly because I didn't even know how to love myself. But God used her to save me. Mila started acting out and got kicked out of two schools in kindergarten, which caused me to have to slow down and face some hard truths. The reality was that she was acting out because she wanted her mama's attention BUT God was using her to get mine. When I was honest with myself that the reason my daughter was having behavioral issues was because I wasn't a present parent, the inner work began, and I was in a prime position to hear God when He called me. Jesus met me in my room at 3am through His Word. He met me in my shame, in my addiction, in my neglect-fulness, in my pain, in my guilt and in my brokenness. . . . He showed me that I am a child. His child. He opened my eyes to see and my ears to hear. He set me free. Truth is, to be able to truly love yourself, your children, and others—you must first have an encounter with Love Himself. It's from our ability to be loved that we can truly and fully love others. Today Mila started the 7th grade. God has kept my baby when I wasn't strong enough to keep her myself. He covered her and shielded her from the darkness that I exposed her to in my ignorance. He will use everything that the enemy meant for bad and turn it for good. God saved me because He loved me and in doing so gave Kamila a mother who could truly love her too. She is my grace and I'm forever grateful.

I had hundreds of comments from moms saying my story was their story too, but they were too ashamed to admit that part of themselves. Women I had never met were commenting that by sharing my story, I unknowingly gave them permission and courage to share theirs.

So why don't we share our stories more often? We've talked at length about silence because of fearing others' opinions, but is there more to our silence than we want to admit? I know you may want me to stop here and say "The end." But I can't. There's one more way shame tries to grip us that we need to talk about.

Sometimes our story remains locked away because we can't handle the emotions and pain that come with our stories. We can.

Shame will tell us we're too much of a mess to share our stories. We're not.

Shame will try to convince us that our emotions disqualify us from sharing our stories. They don't.

Shame lies and insists that if we're still in pain, our stories have no power. They do.

I remember when this last remnant of shame showed up in my life.

Am I not healed? was the thought that raced through my head as I was sharing a part of my story with a friend while we watched her children run freely through the playground, laughing and calling out for their mama to see them go down the slide. I gripped my son's stroller as though it was giving me the strength and support I needed to get through the story I was telling.

Tears began to well up in my eyes and my voice began to shake as I explained how it felt to grow up with shelter and more than enough food but not the emotional support my tender heart needed. It took a long time for me to realize my dad was a great provider of physical necessities, but as a young girl growing up without a mom in our home, I needed validation, affirmation, and physical nurturing that he didn't know how to provide. I spent years feeling unwanted and doubting my worth. In talking about it, I felt the pain all over again.

As humans, we are programmed to reject pain and avoid it at all costs. We have been taught that happiness is the main goal in life, but that simply is not true. For most of my life, I pretended to be happy to make those around me more comfortable, but I've learned it's in my pain and brokenness that God meets me, comforts me, and gives me beauty for my ashes (Isaiah 61:3). When I allow my brokenness to draw me closer to Him, I sense His presence come closer to me, just as the psalmist wrote: "The LORD is close to the brokenhearted and saves those who are crushed in spirit" (Psalm 34:18).

That day at the playground, every emotion was tangible as I explained that I learned early on that having no emotional needs was the only way to survive. As I shared this intimate part of my story in response to the simple question she had asked me moments earlier, I realized I wasn't crying because I felt bad for myself; I was crying because I had allowed myself to stay tender to my pain and brokenness.

The question my friend had asked that started the flow of emotions and tears was a seemingly easy one: "What's the heart behind She Speaks Fire?" My honest answer was one that I had fought a lifetime to accept. To truly know the heart behind my ministry, the root had to be revealed. And the root of my story, my life message, and my ministry was and is summed up in two words: *shame* and *pain*.

I know God uses the pain I carry deep down to birth something beautiful in me every day, which I am now able to give others. My pain has become my calling. I have a burden for people who are hurting, living in brokenness, and without hope. I wake up every day with a fire in my heart and spirit to introduce them to the only One who has the power to set them free.

Even though God delivered me from the spirit of heaviness and defeat, the memories are still there, but instead of feeling hopeless, I am reminded to give glory to Jesus, who rescued me from that darkness. Every time I feel the familiar tug of pain or the tears creep into the corners of my eyes, I know they carry the power to heal both me and others. They both work together for my good, and the truth of the promise in Romans becomes more than just words on a page: "And we know that all things work together for good to those who love God, to those who are called according to His purpose" (8:28 NKJV).

I have an unpopular stance on pain and brokenness—I embrace them both. See, I relate to pain much more than I know how to relate to happiness.

I've encountered some who believe that evidence of our healing is being able to reflect on our pain without being moved by feelings and emotions. I wonder how many people have kept their stories hidden because of that lie. I've come to realize through this Genesis journey in the garden that our pain needs to be addressed and managed, just like everything else in our lives. It would be so much easier to dissociate and bury the shame and pain down deep, but our ability to stay tender to our pain is what helps us stay tender to the pain of others.

Those who experience pain can still smile and those who have battled shame for years can still hope.

Being saved and having a relationship with Jesus doesn't always take away the pain that we carry in the deepest parts of us, and that's okay. His grace carries us and all we're carrying in the midst of it. So instead of running from pain, denying it, sitting in it, or flat-out putting up a front like it's completely gone, I stay tender to it. Don't be fooled. I am not a superwoman who has it all together; I am a broken woman who knows the One who makes me whole.

Throughout this book I have shared my story to bring God glory and to battle shame head-on. Shame will not have the final say, and I will no longer hide in fear, and neither should you.

We all have a message that God has given us to share with our generation that burns within. The fire you carry has been kindled from the unique experiences of your life;

the ups and downs, the valleys and the mountaintops, the pain, the joy, the success, and the failures all speak. They testify and bear witness to something we all have in common: what it is to be human and what it is to know God.

We are the body of Christ, and the mission and message in our story to tell the world about Jesus must go on. Jesus came to save the lost, and He's doing that now through you and me. We are called to be witnesses to the world. We are called to own our stories and share our stories—without shame, without fear, and without hesitation.

We are called to own our stories and share our stories— without shame, without fear, and without hesitation.

You have been hiding, but God is calling you.

You have been crying among the trees, but God is calling you.

You have been sewing fig leaves over your shame, but God is calling you.

Now go. It's time for you to get up and start speaking fire.

Acknowledgments

Writing this book was one of the hardest things I have ever done in my life, but I believe God used this process to show me just how truly loved and supported I really am, for that I am grateful.

Thank you to my family, who was with me in the trenches during this process—from beginning to end. To my three babies, my mom, my dad, and my sisters: I love you more than words can express. Thank you for always believing the best in me and reminding me of who I was when my vision was blurry. Thank you for speaking life into me when the pressure almost took me out. I wouldn't have been able to do this without your love and support.

To my friends—Brittni De La Mora, Josephine Rose, Bethny Ricks, Cassandra Speer, Amy Klutinoty, Jackie Aviles, Ashley Robbins, Kara Stout, Brittany Maher, Charaia Rush, and Amber Wilson—who prayed for me through this whole process. Each of you stood alongside me and held my arms up when my strength was dwindling. For that and so much more, thank you. I now understand more deeply that it is not the quantity of friends but the quality of the meaningful few that God blesses us with that truly matters. You are my people and I love you.

To my pastors, TJ and Carissa Anglin, who made themselves available to me when I needed support. Thank you both for making any and every resource available to me so that nothing hindered my voice and calling. Thank you for opening the office for me to come write when the noise in my home with two small children proved too chaotic. Your support, your grace, and the way you champion my life and calling is unmatched.

To Leticia Ventura, who has been in the background for many years making the voices of others known through her work in unseen places. You have offered your gifts as a sacrifice unto the Lord for the work He is doing through the lives of others while being content with making much of Jesus and not wanting glory for yourself. Thank you for believing in this message and for being a set of faithful eyes that guided me through this process. I am so grateful for you.

To Janet Talbert, who proved to be the gift I didn't know I needed through every step of this journey. Thank God He knew exactly who I needed as my editor. Thank you for your kindness toward me at each mountaintop and valley. Thank you for the words of affirmation you continued to echo to my heart when I would become weary and doubted

ACKNOWLEDGMENTS

I could even write a book. You were so gentle with me as you combed through the words that poured out of my heart. God hooked me up with you, and I love you very much.

To my She Speaks Fire community, who has fueled the fire in my soul for this book. Thank you for the privilege of serving you all these years. This book is the fruit of this ministry and wouldn't exist without the culture of transparency and authenticity that you have helped create. Thank you for trusting me to speak the word of God over you and for supporting me all these years as we journeyed together through the ups and downs of life. I love you with all my heart and am ready for so much more to come!

Notes

1. *Merriam-Webster*, s.v. "shame," accessed July 18, 2023, https://www.merriam-webster.com/dictionary/shame.
2. E. A. Gassin, quoted in *Baker Encyclopedia of Psychology & Counseling*, 2nd ed., ed. David G. Benner and Peter C. Hill (Grand Rapids: Baker Books, 1999), 604.
3. Chad Brand, Charles Draper, and Archie England, eds., *Holman Illustrated Bible Dictionary*, s.v. "apple of the eye" (Nashville: Holman Bible Publishers, 2003), 90.
4. *Strong's Concordance*, s.v. "Aischuné: shame," Bible Hub, accessed September 29, 2023, https://biblehub.com/greek /152.htm.
5. William Smith, *Smith's Bible Dictionary*, s.v. "man" (Philadelphia: A.J. Holman Company, 1901).
6. *Oxford Dictionary of English*, 3rd ed. (Oxford: Oxford University Press, 2010), s.v. "crafty."
7. Sun Tzu, *The Art of War*, trans. Lionel Giles (Sweden: Wisehouse Classics, 2020), 14.

About the Author

Mariela Rosario is a writer, coach, and spoken word artist. In 2015 Mariela had a radical encounter with God, and since then she has dedicated her life to helping others be the best version of themselves and walk in their God-given purpose. She has a bachelor's degree in Christian ministries and founded She Speaks Fire (shespeaksfire.com) in 2018, which has grown to be an international ministry impacting thousands of souls daily for Christ through its digital resources, courses, podcast, and social media. She speaks at conferences and various church events with the hope of making Jesus known and God glorified. Mariela and her family live in San Diego, California.